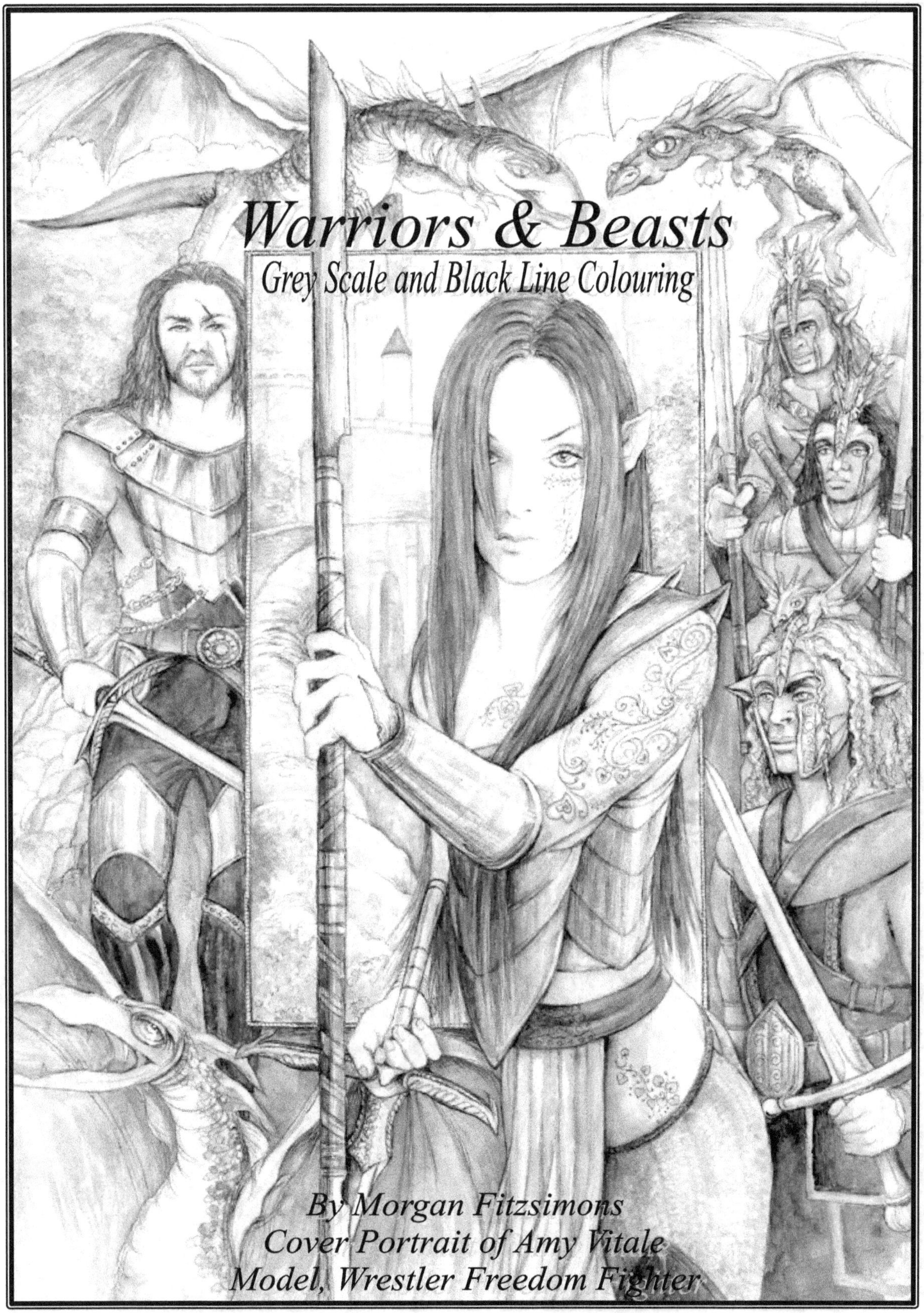

# Warriors & Beasts
## Grey Scale and Black Line Colouring

*By Morgan Fitzsimons*
*Cover Portrait of Amy Vitale*
*Model, Wrestler Freedom Fighter*

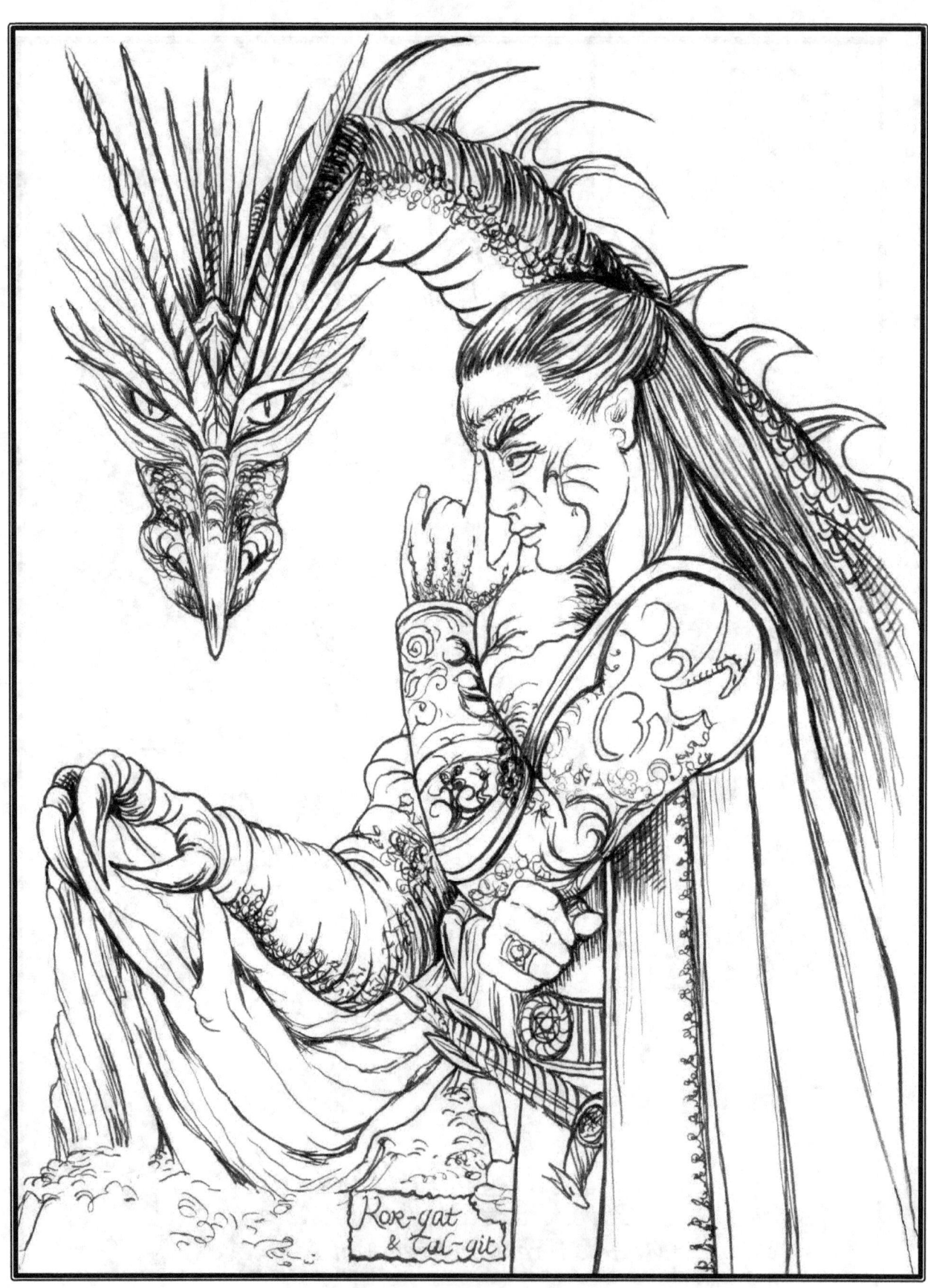

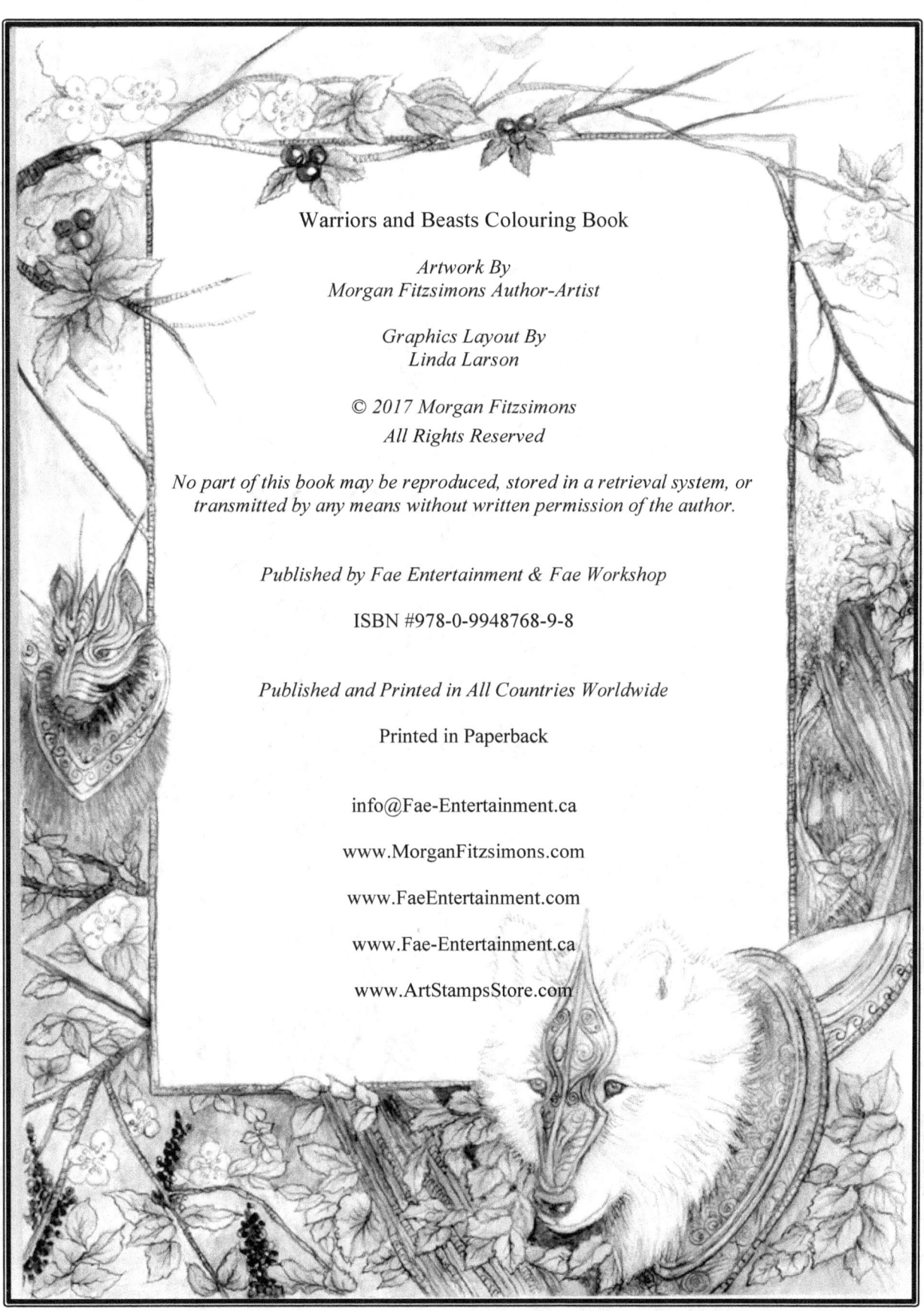

Warriors and Beasts Colouring Book

*Artwork By*
*Morgan Fitzsimons Author-Artist*

*Graphics Layout By*
*Linda Larson*

*Published by Fae Entertainment & Fae Workshop*

ISBN #978-0-9948768-9-8

*Published and Printed in All Countries Worldwide*

Printed in Paperback

info@Fae-Entertainment.ca

www.MorganFitzsimons.com

www.FaeEntertainment.com

www.Fae-Entertainment.ca

www.ArtStampsStore.com

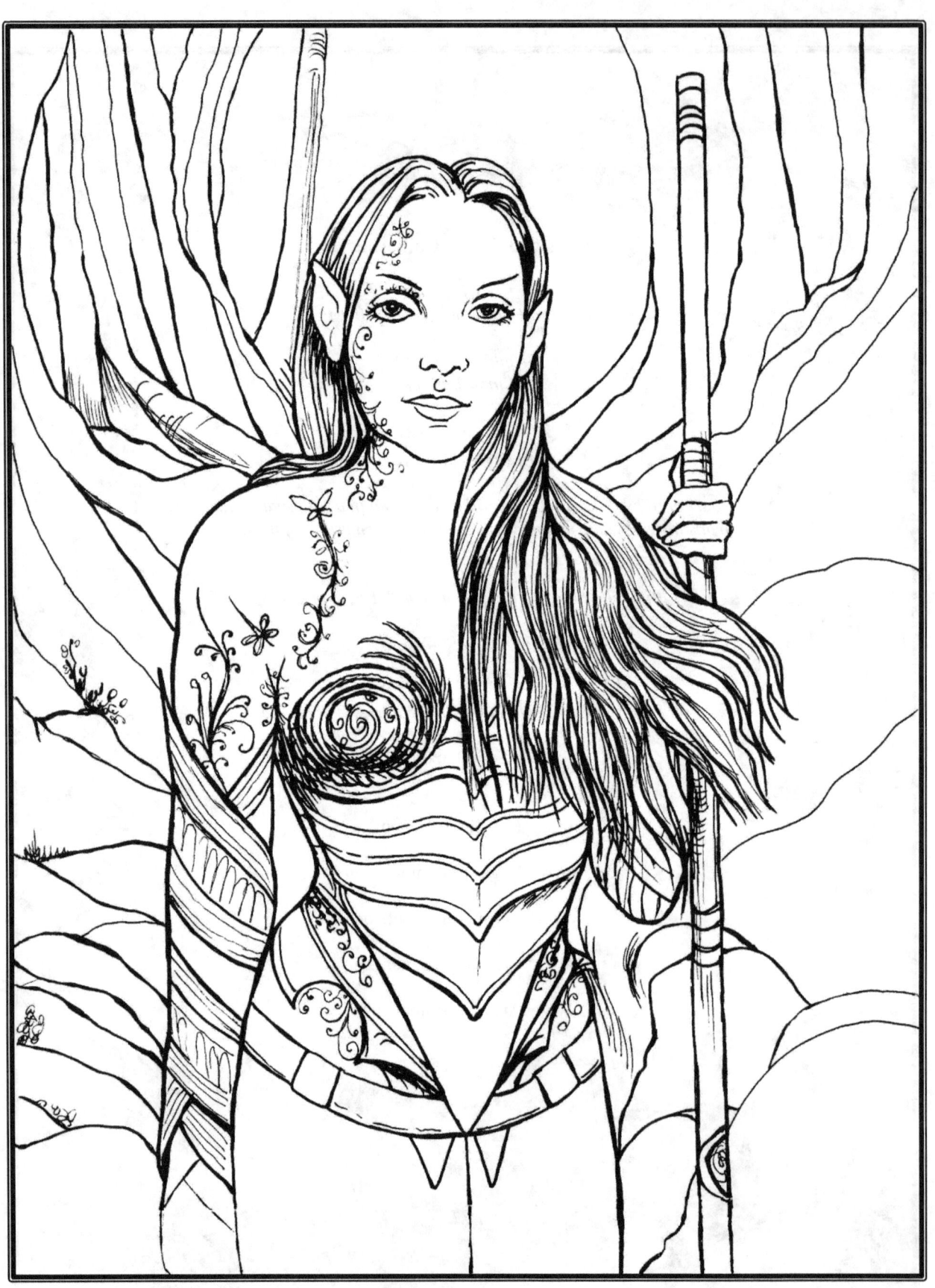

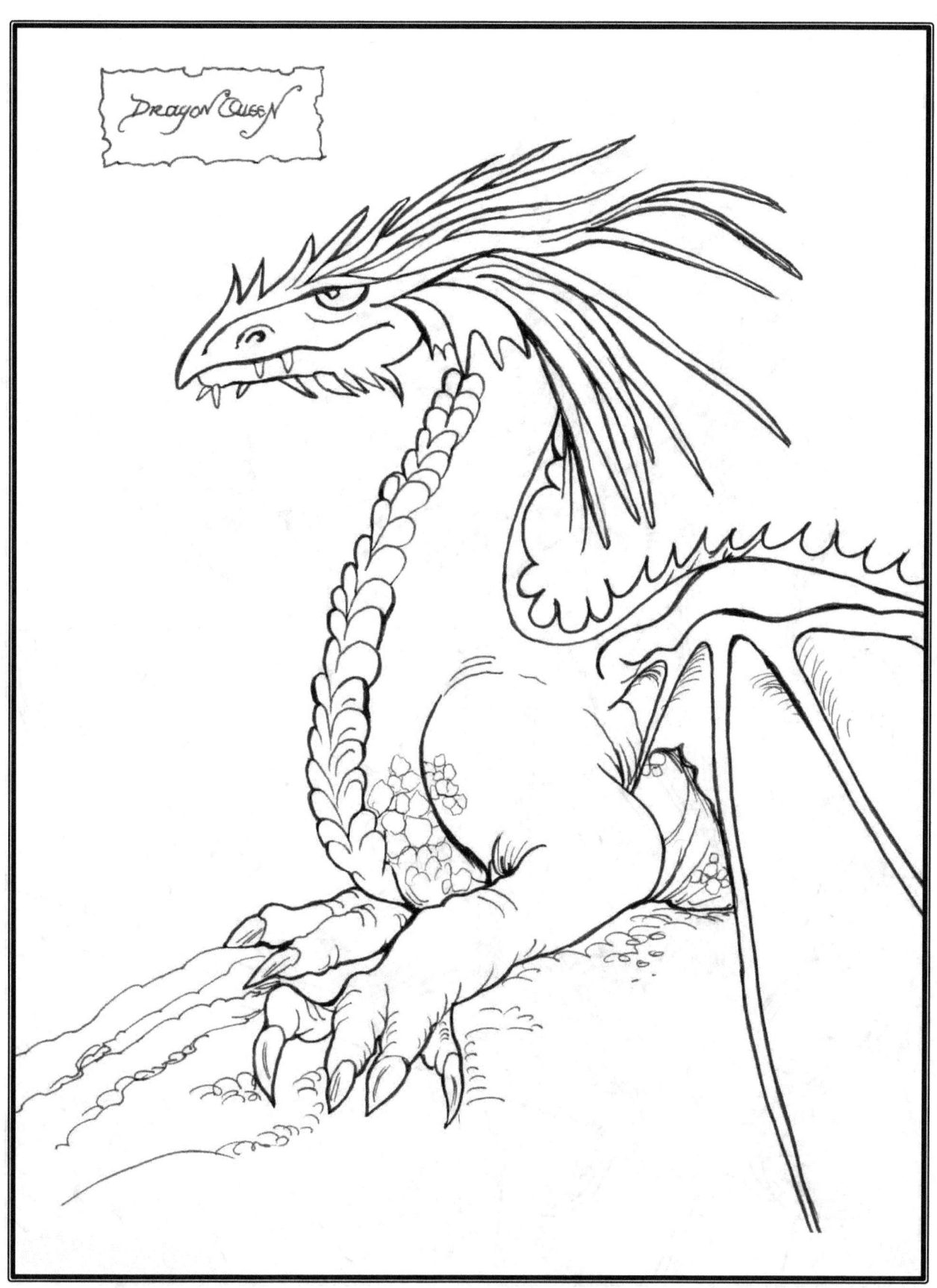

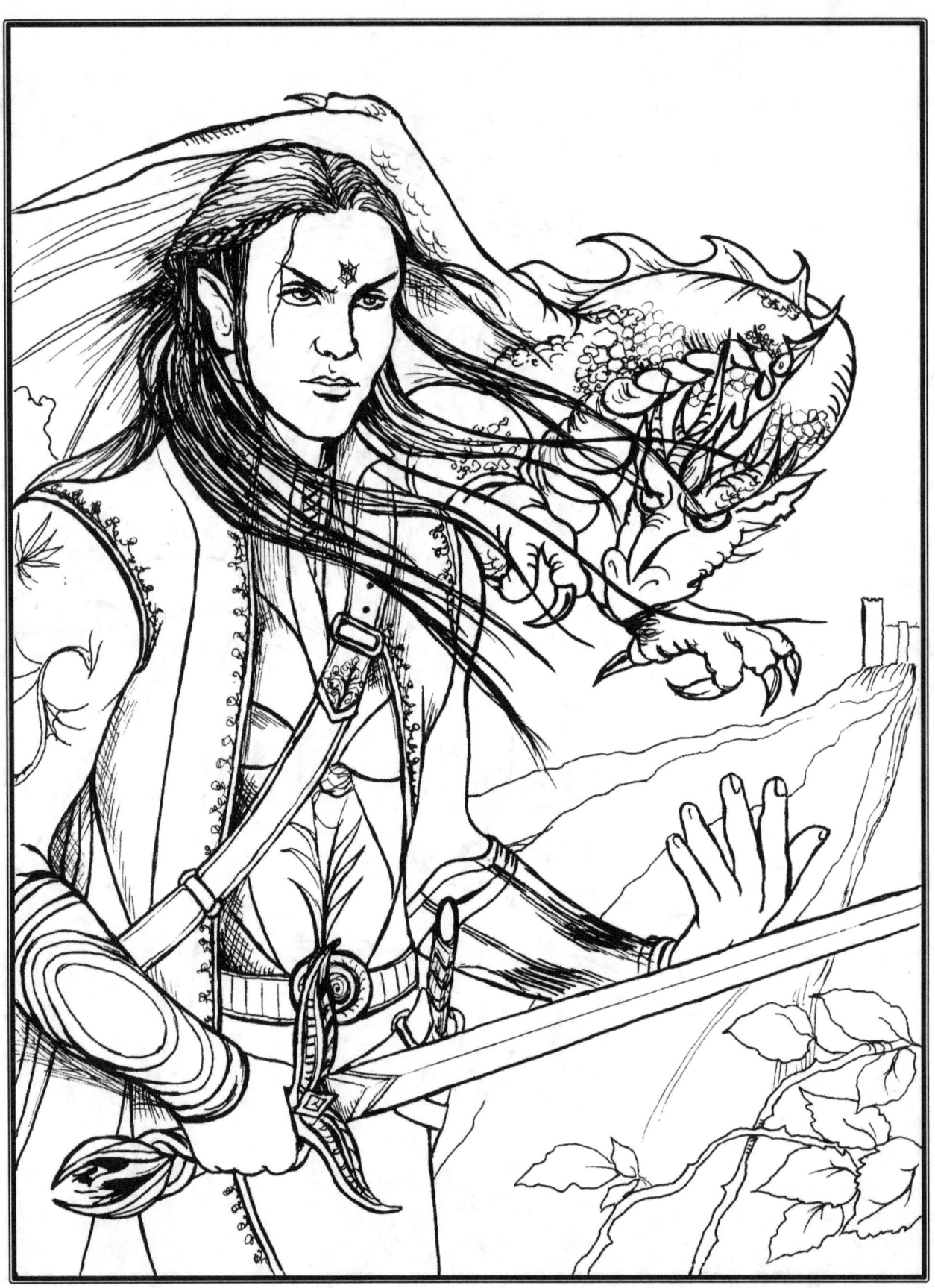

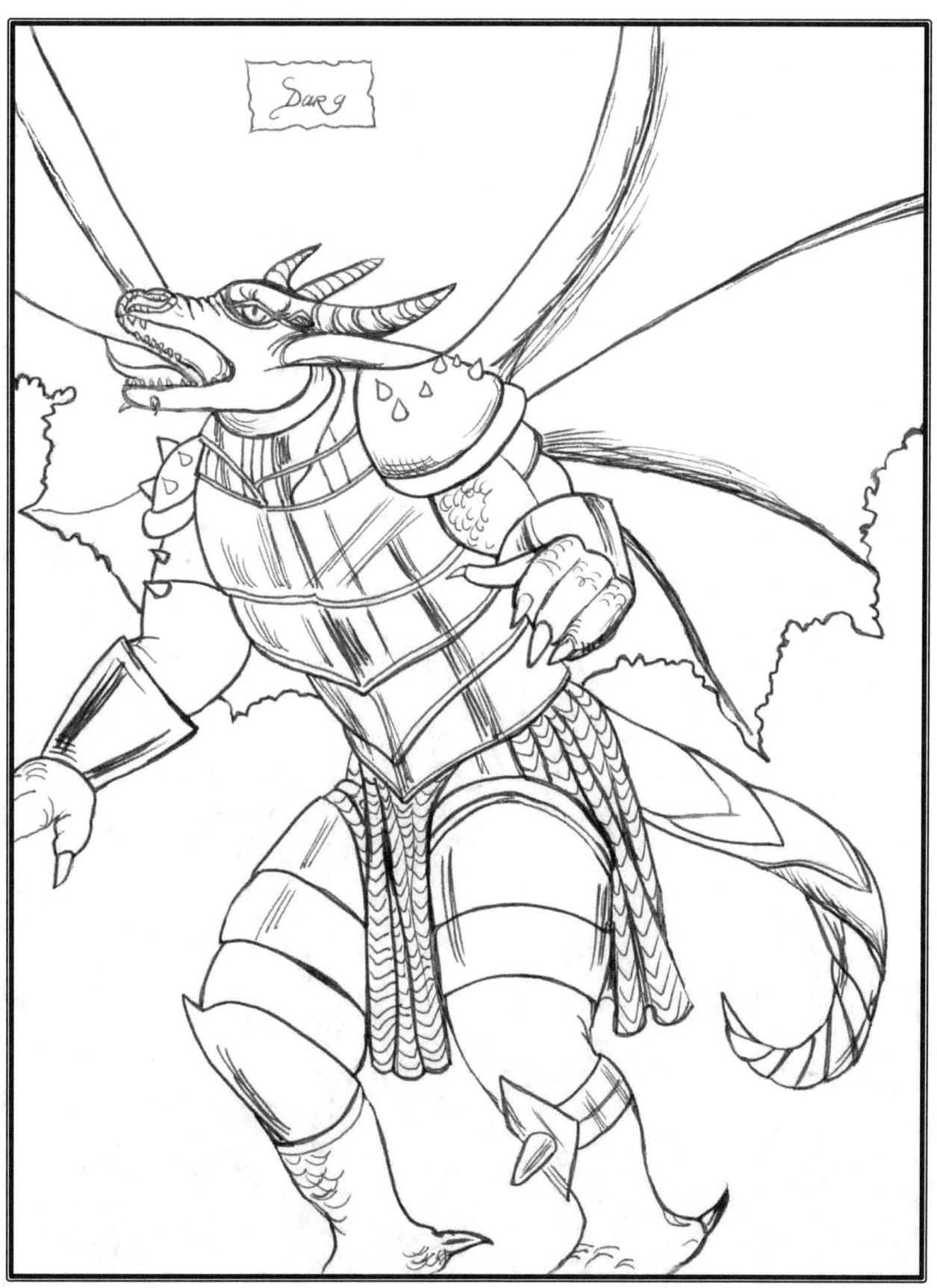
Darg

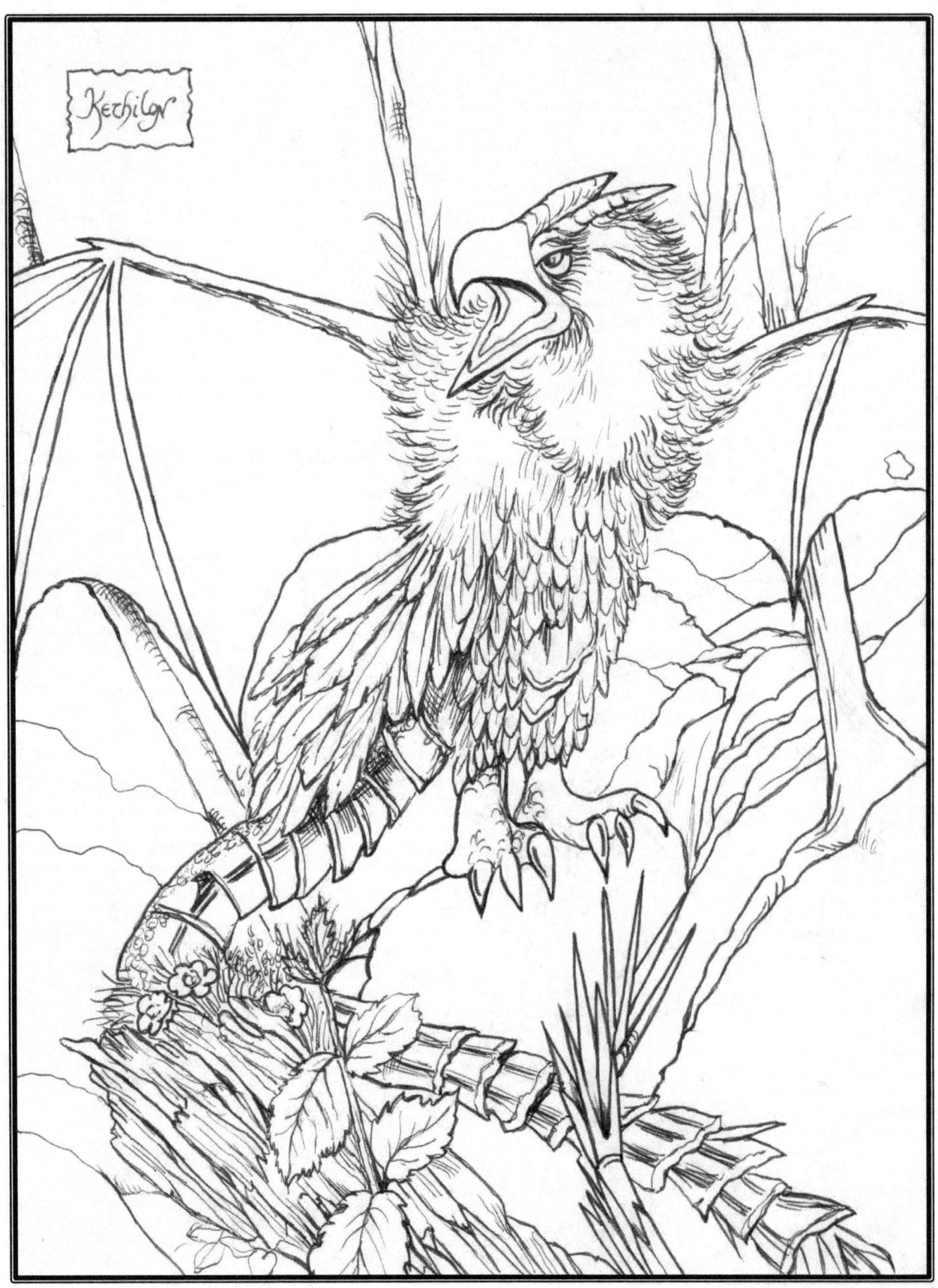

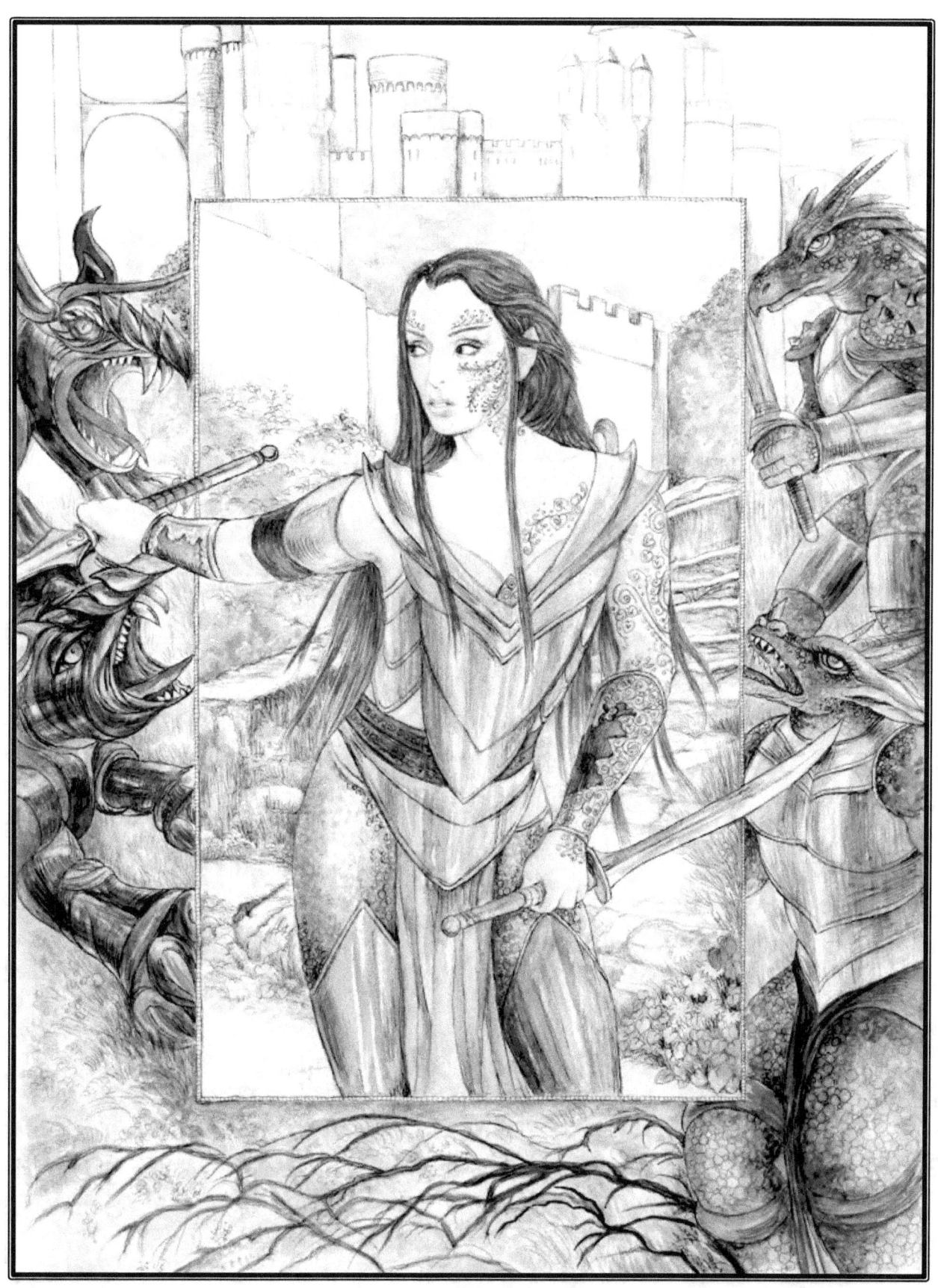

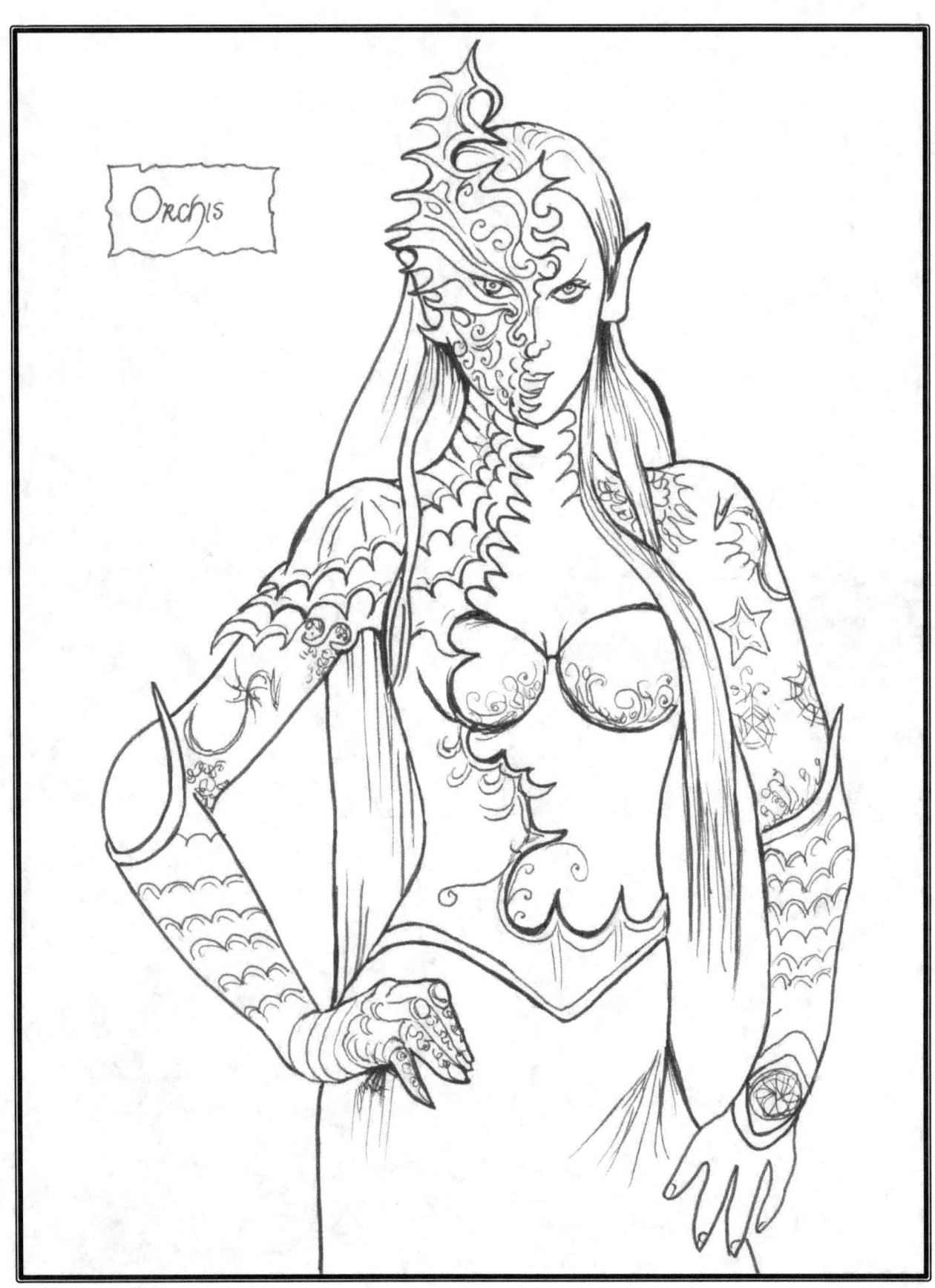

Orchis

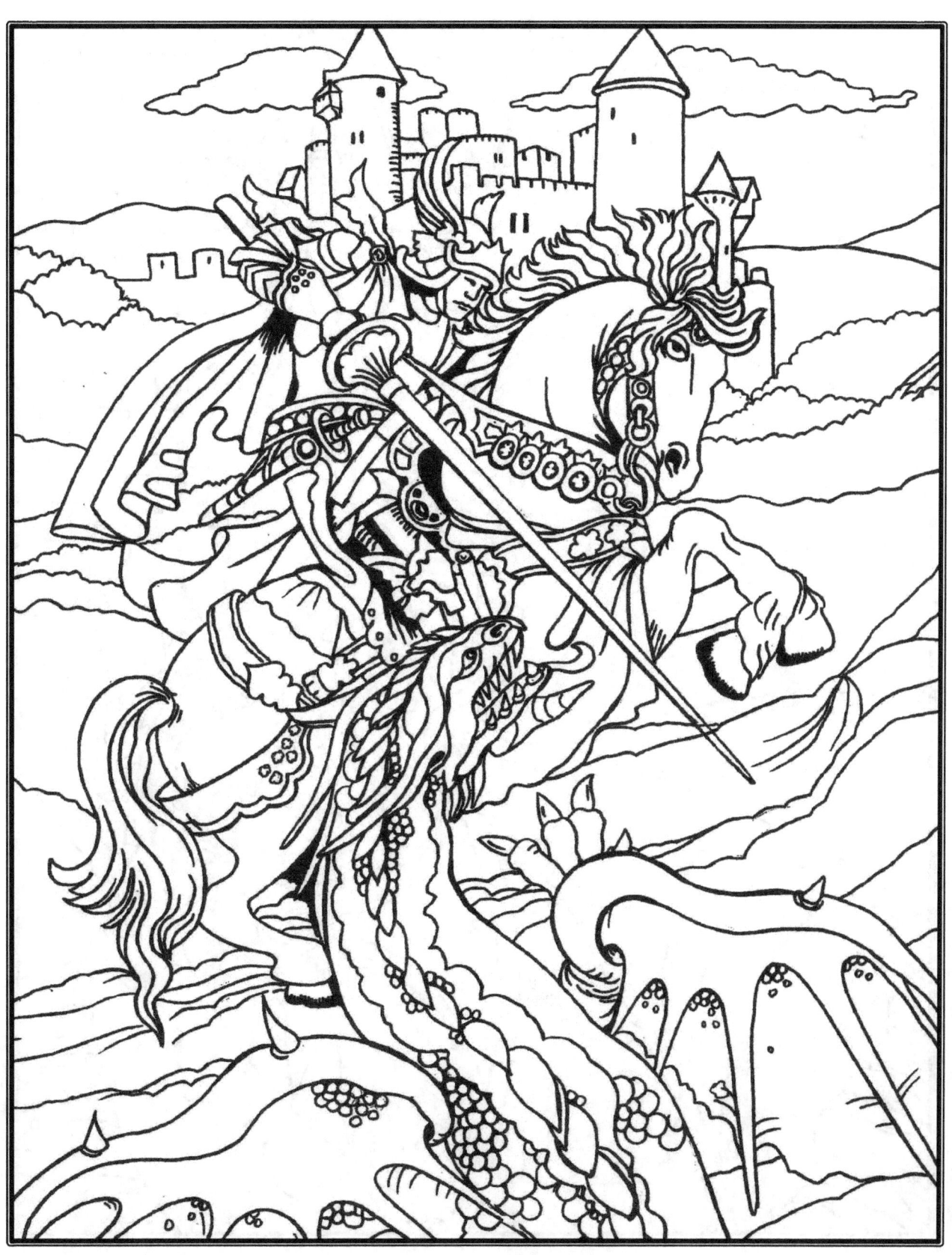

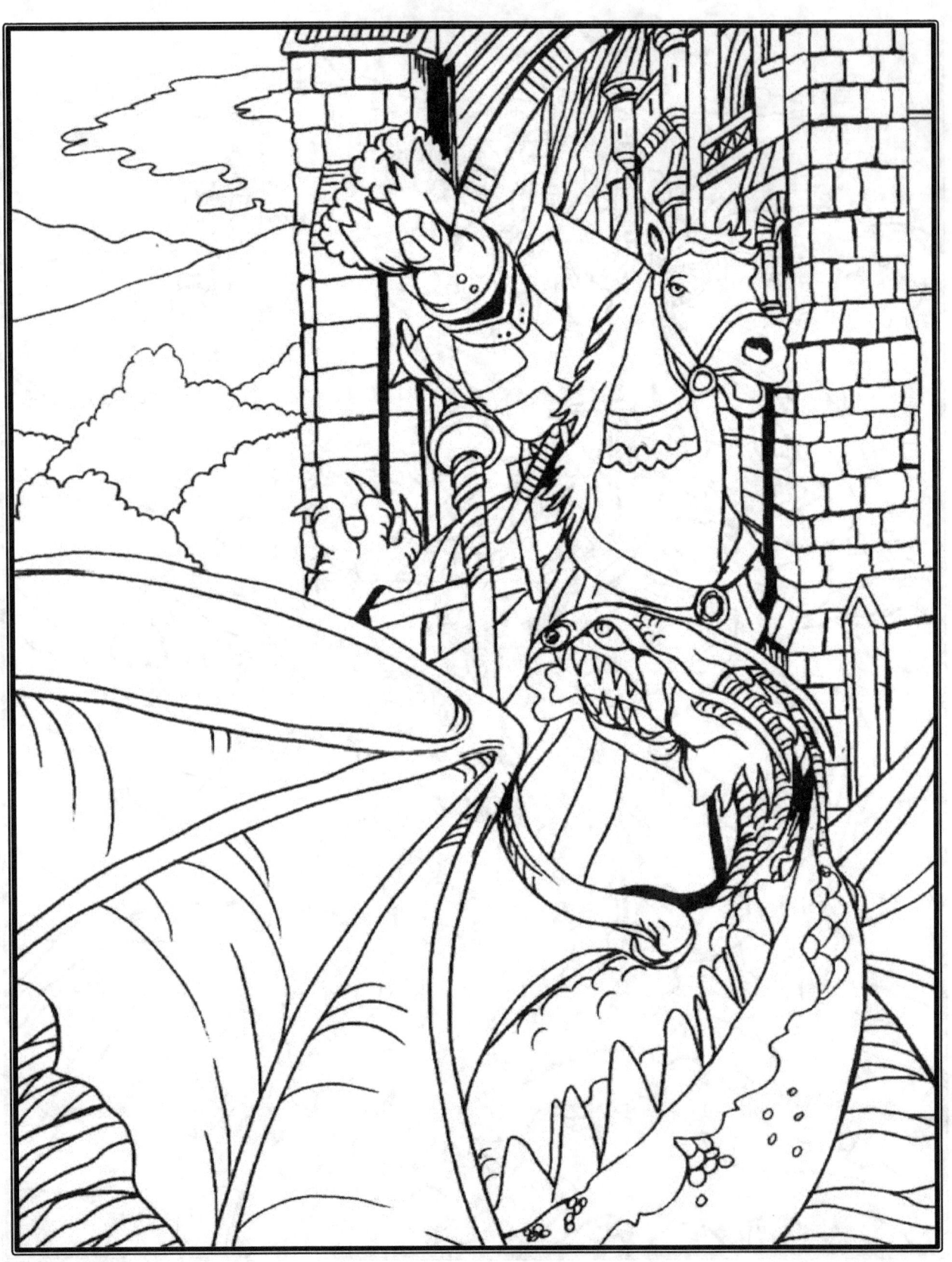

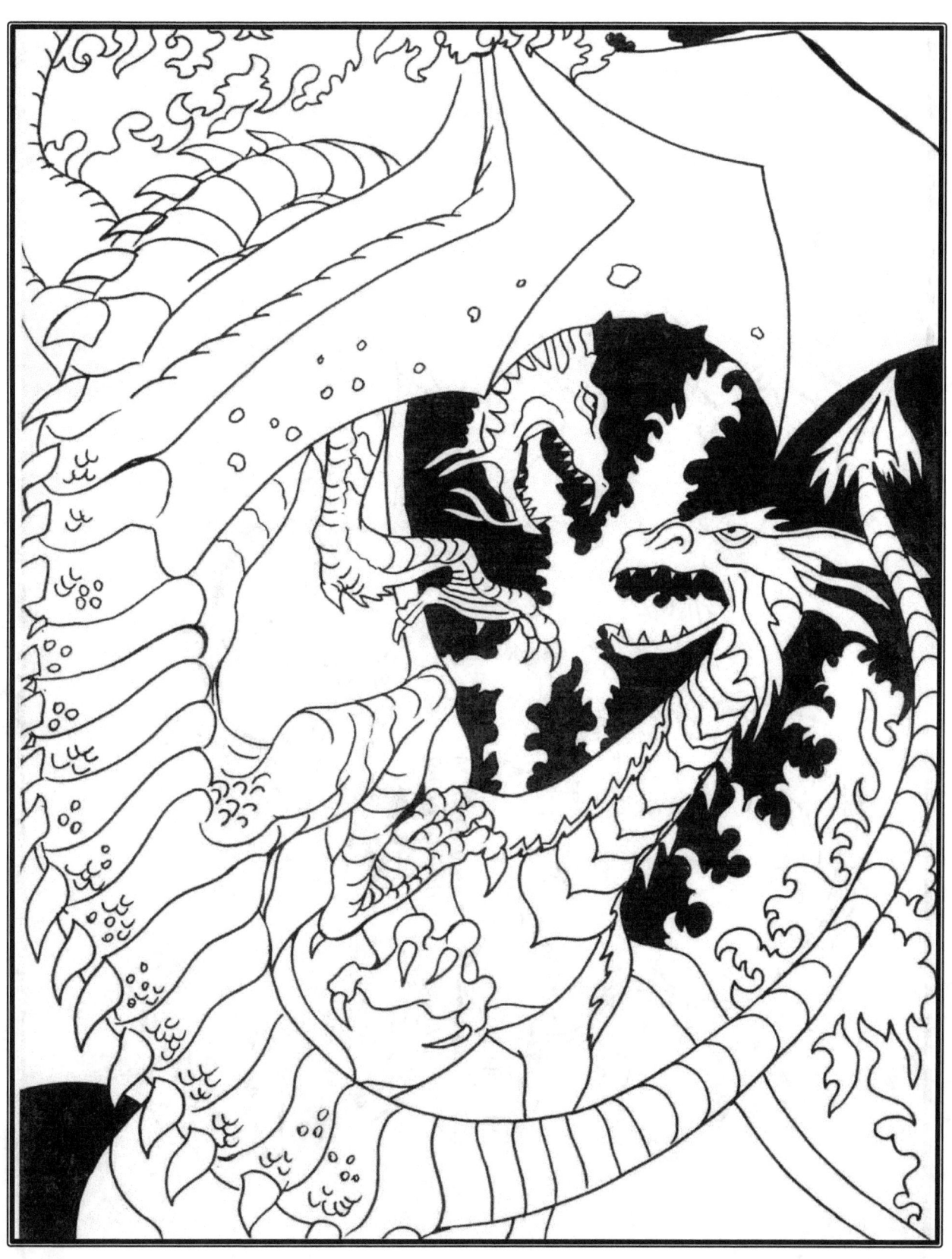

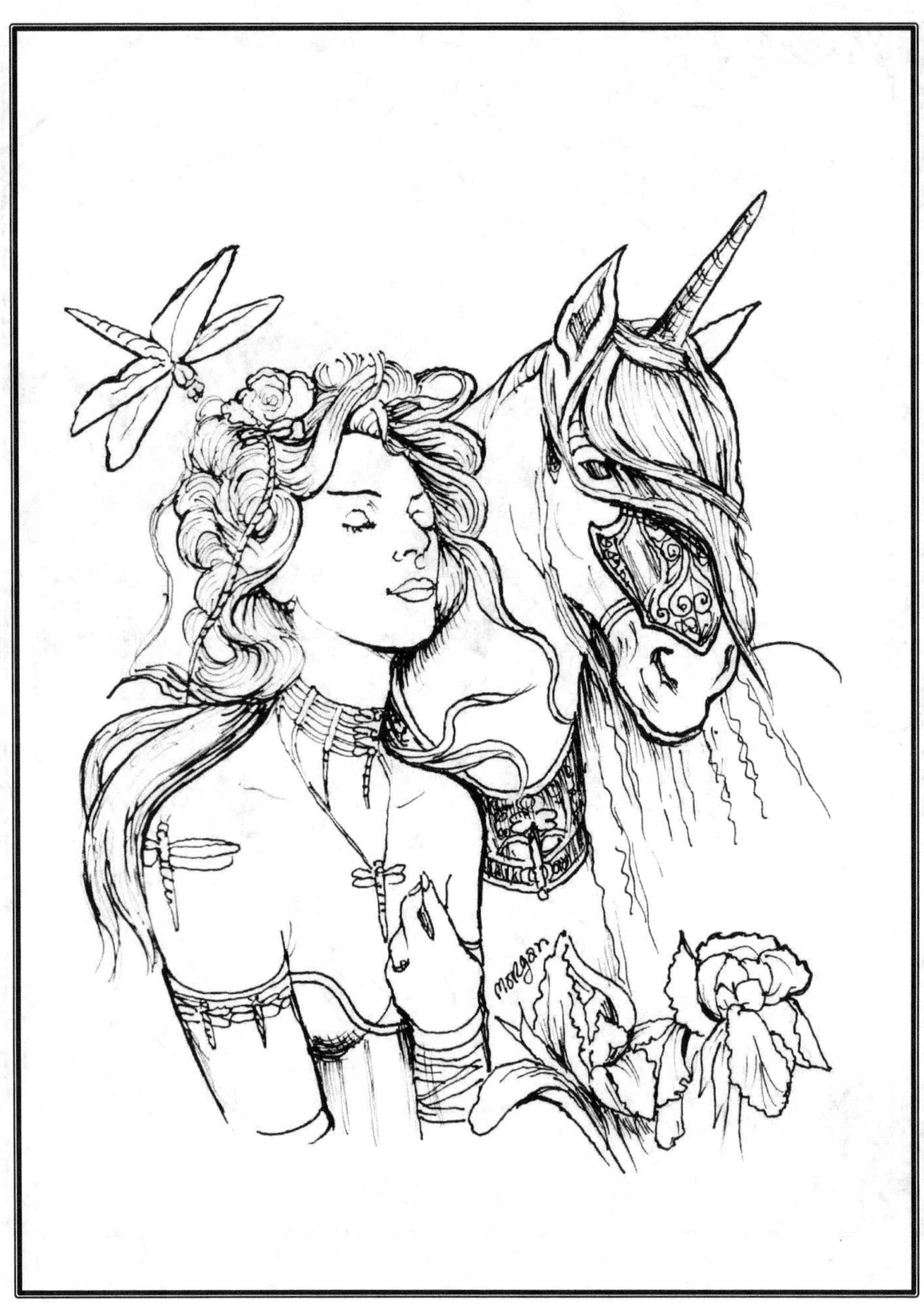

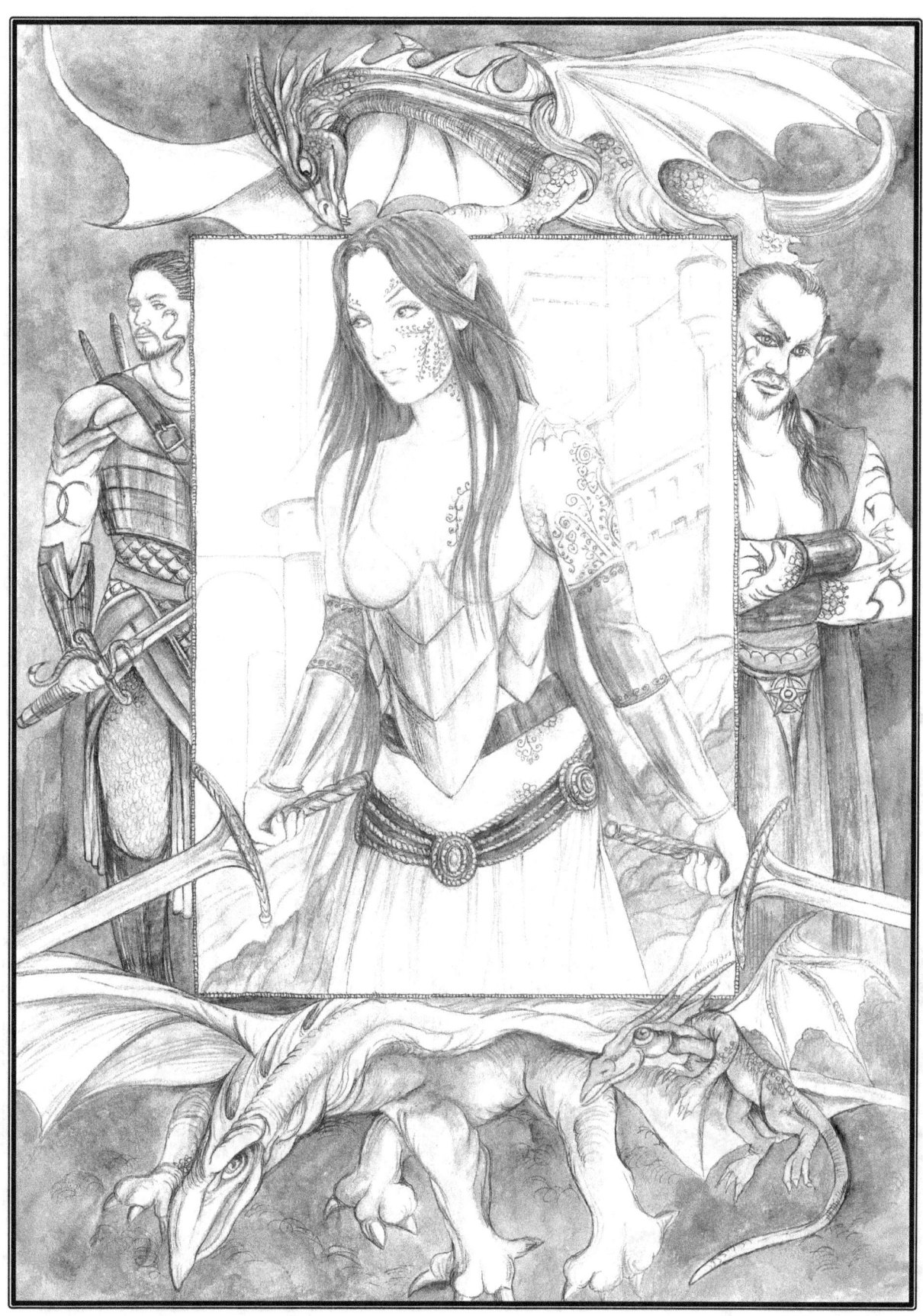

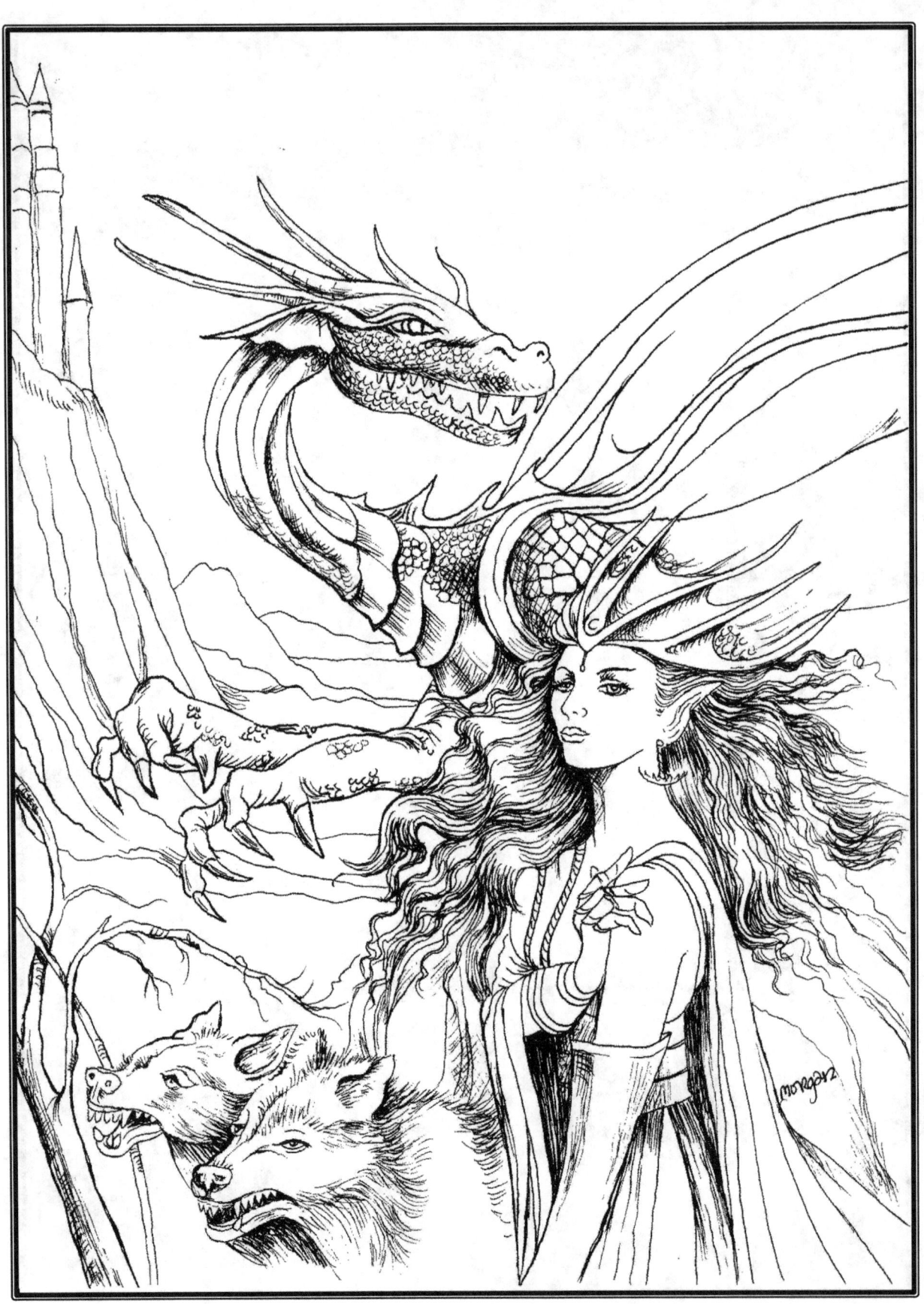

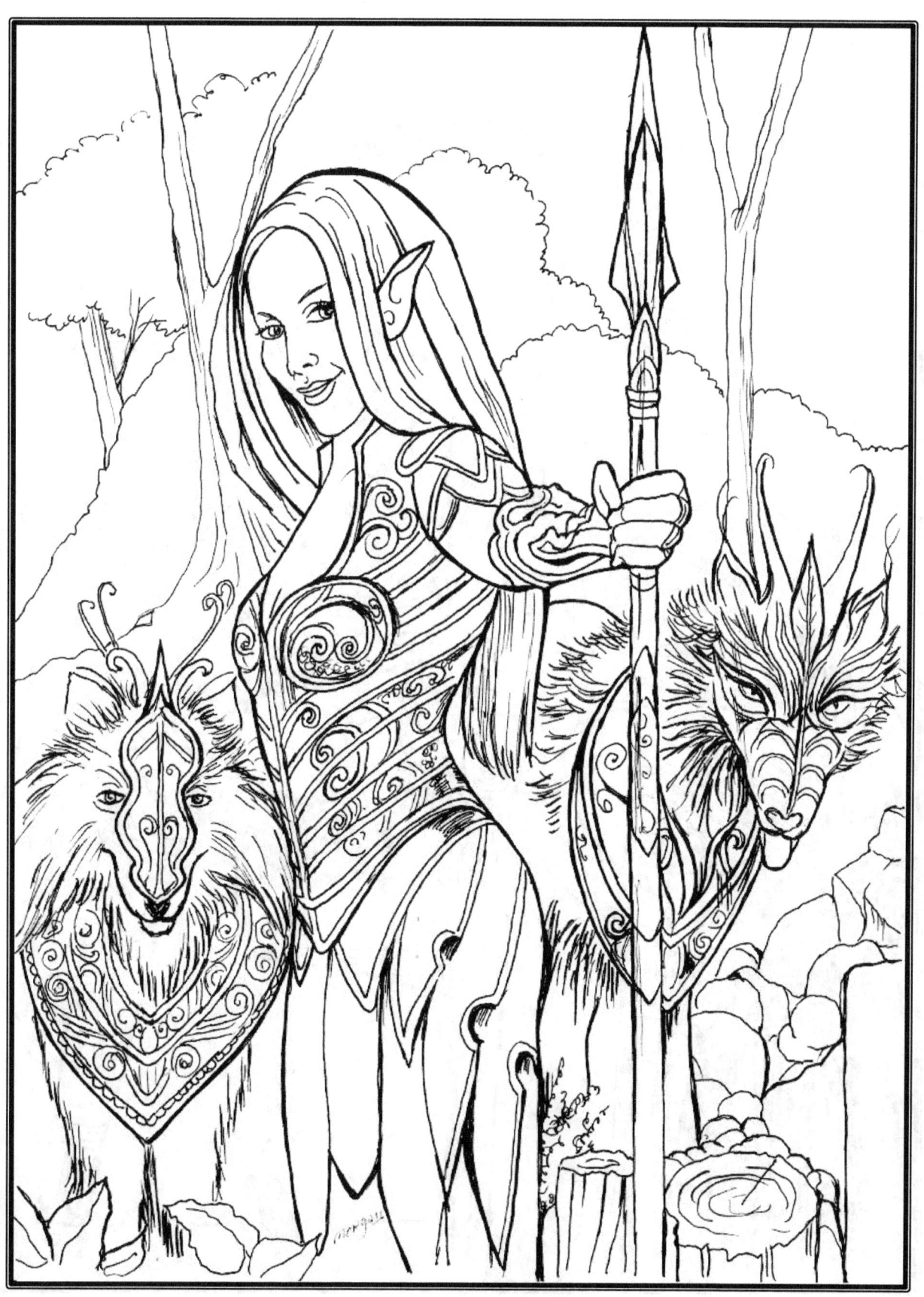

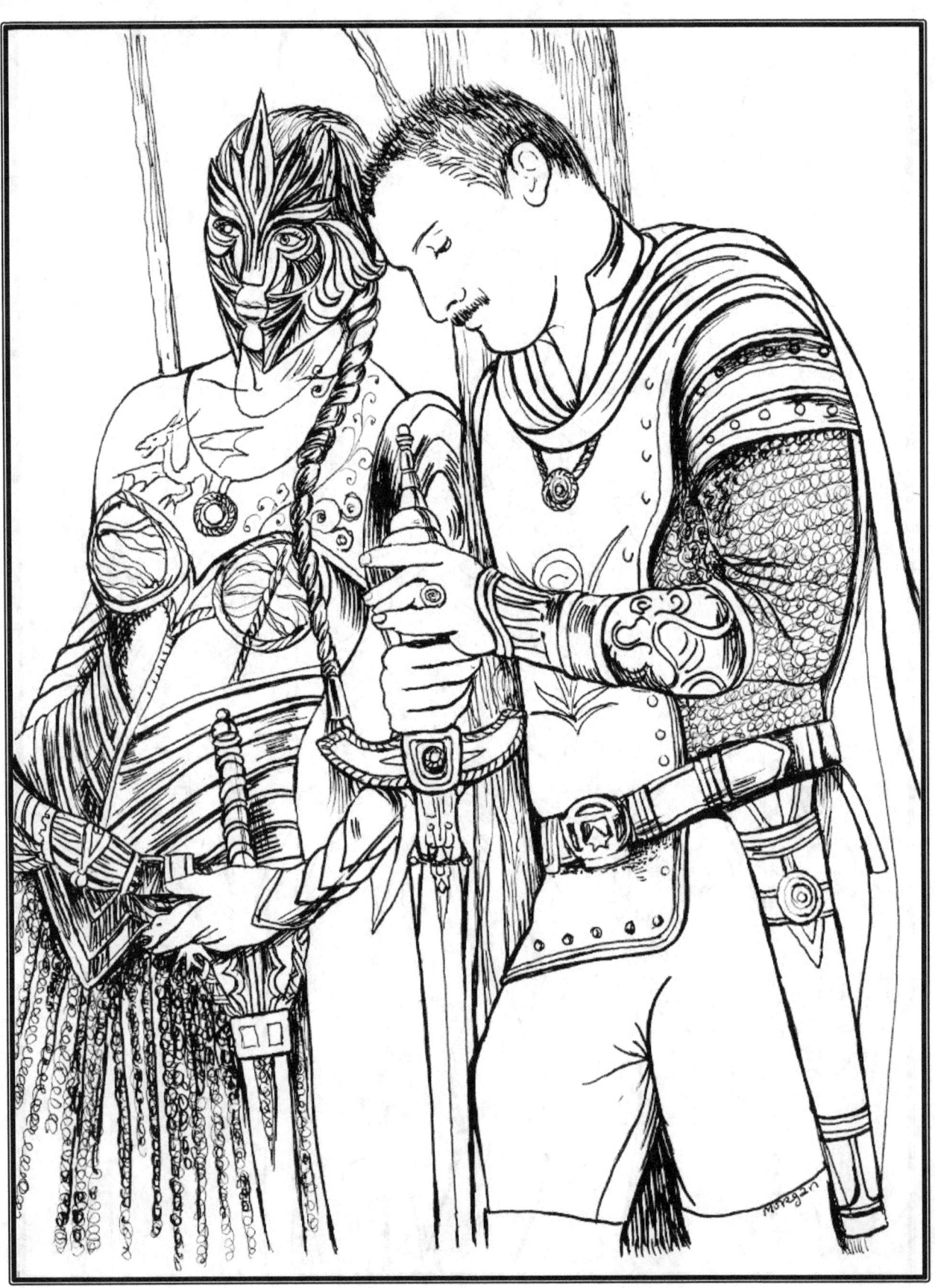

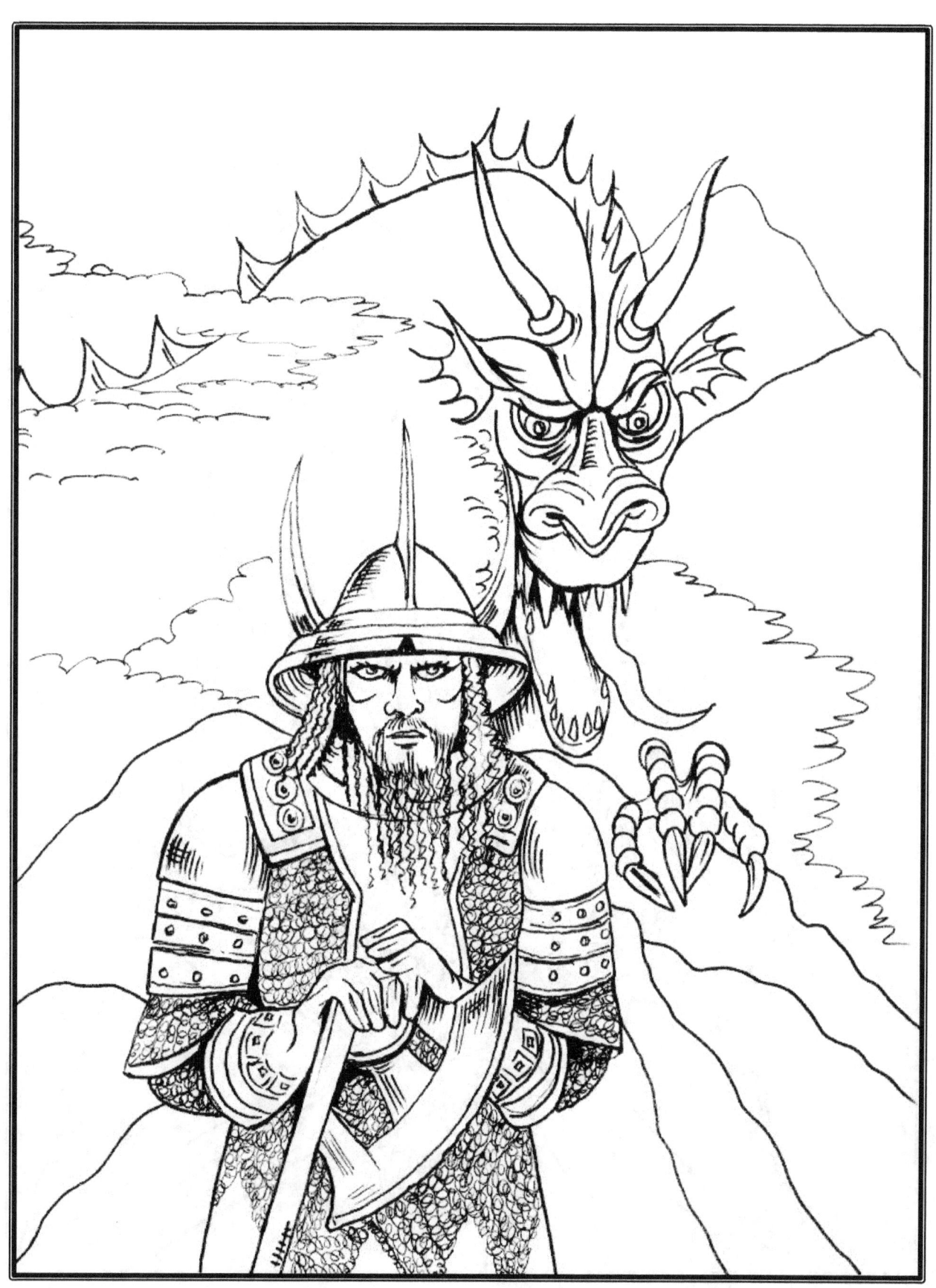

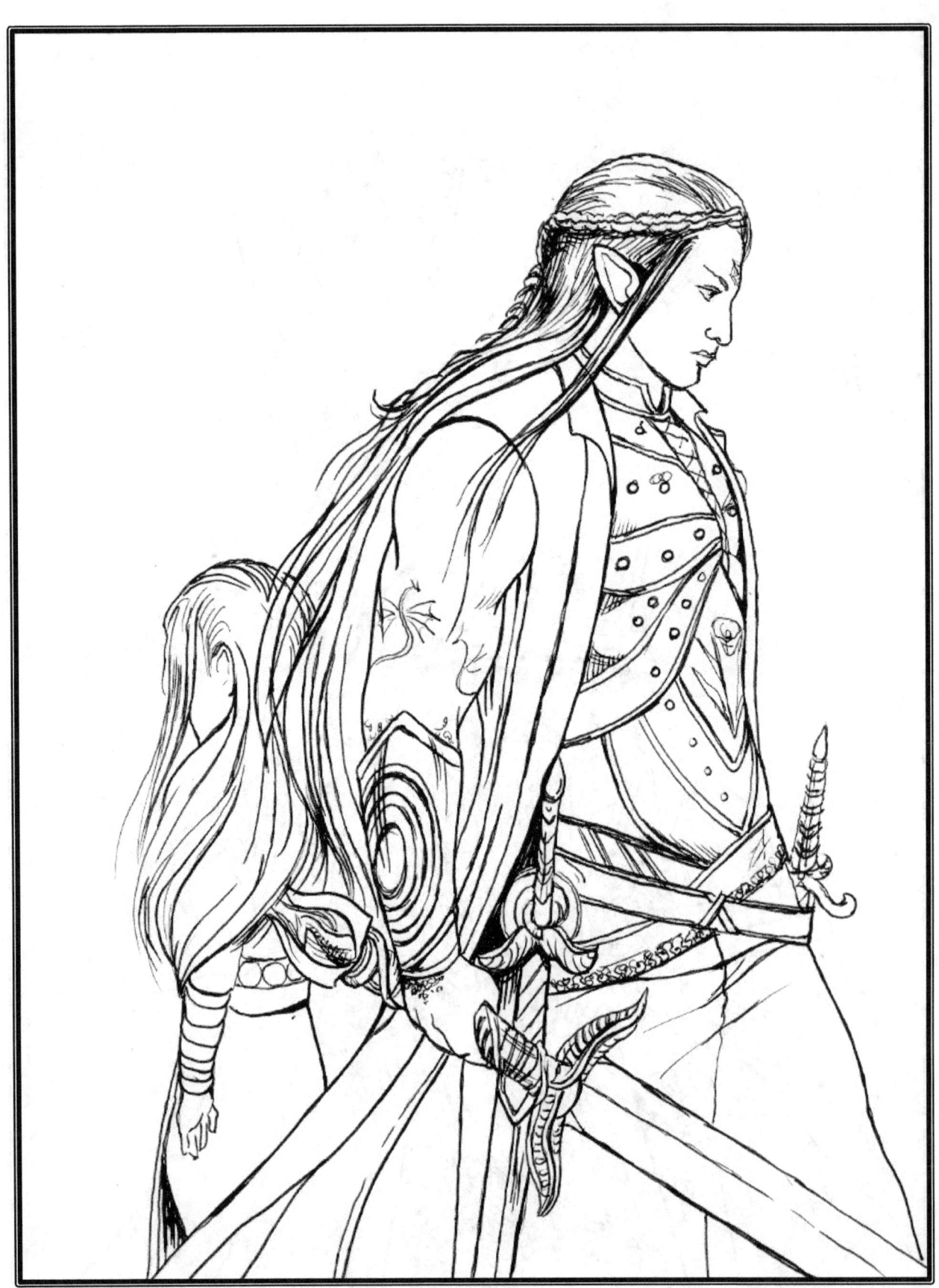

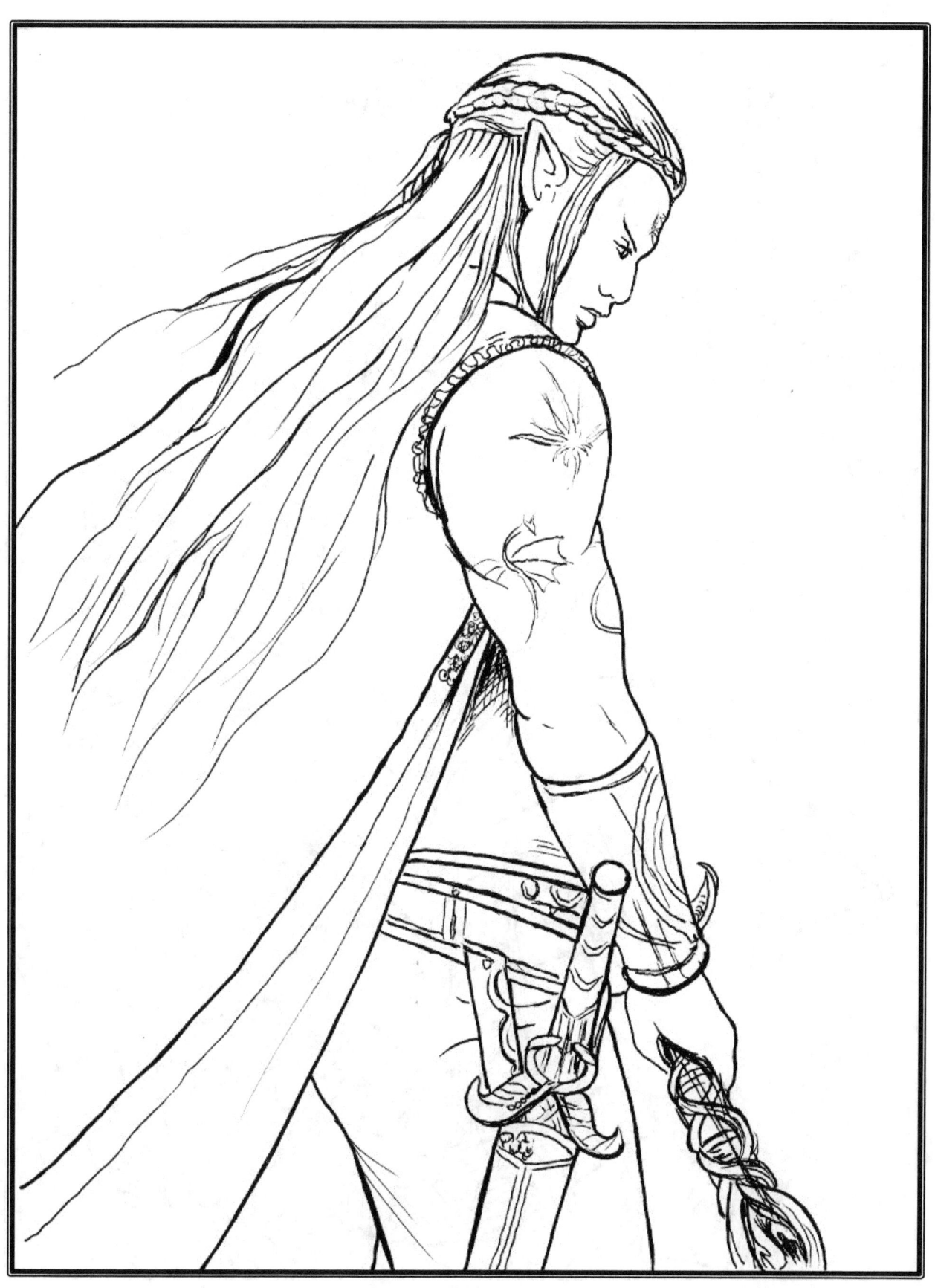

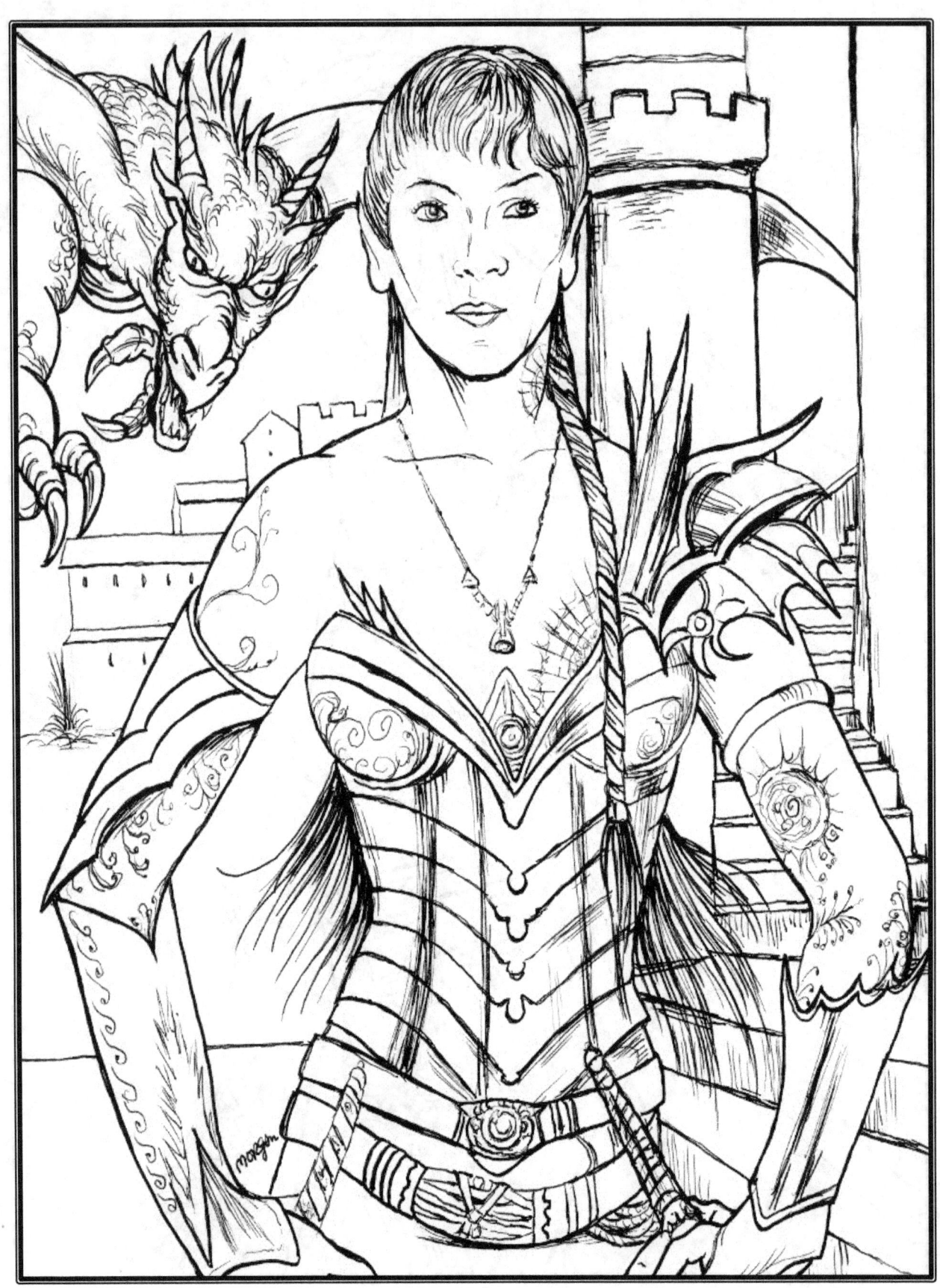

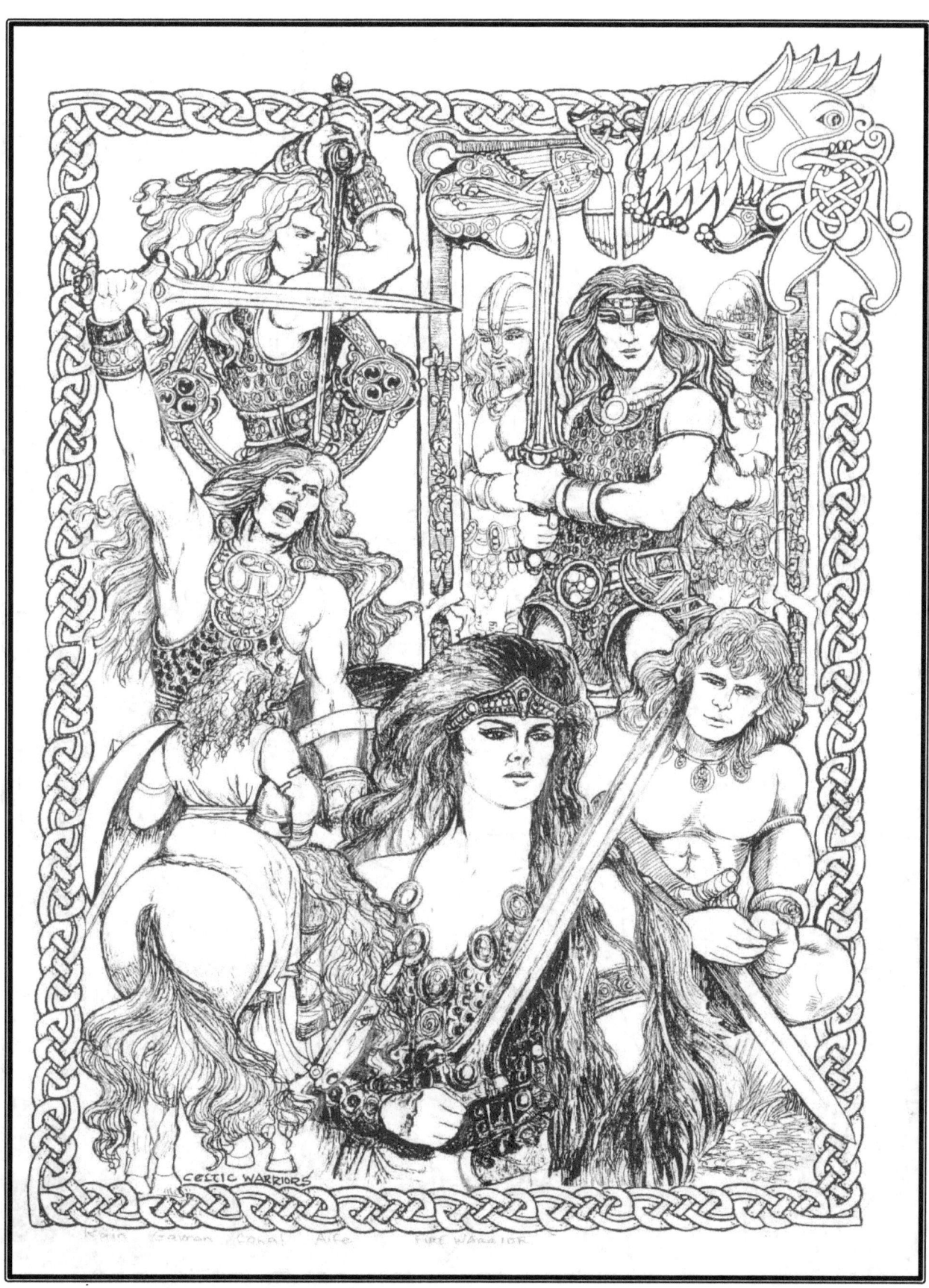

CELTIC WARRIORS

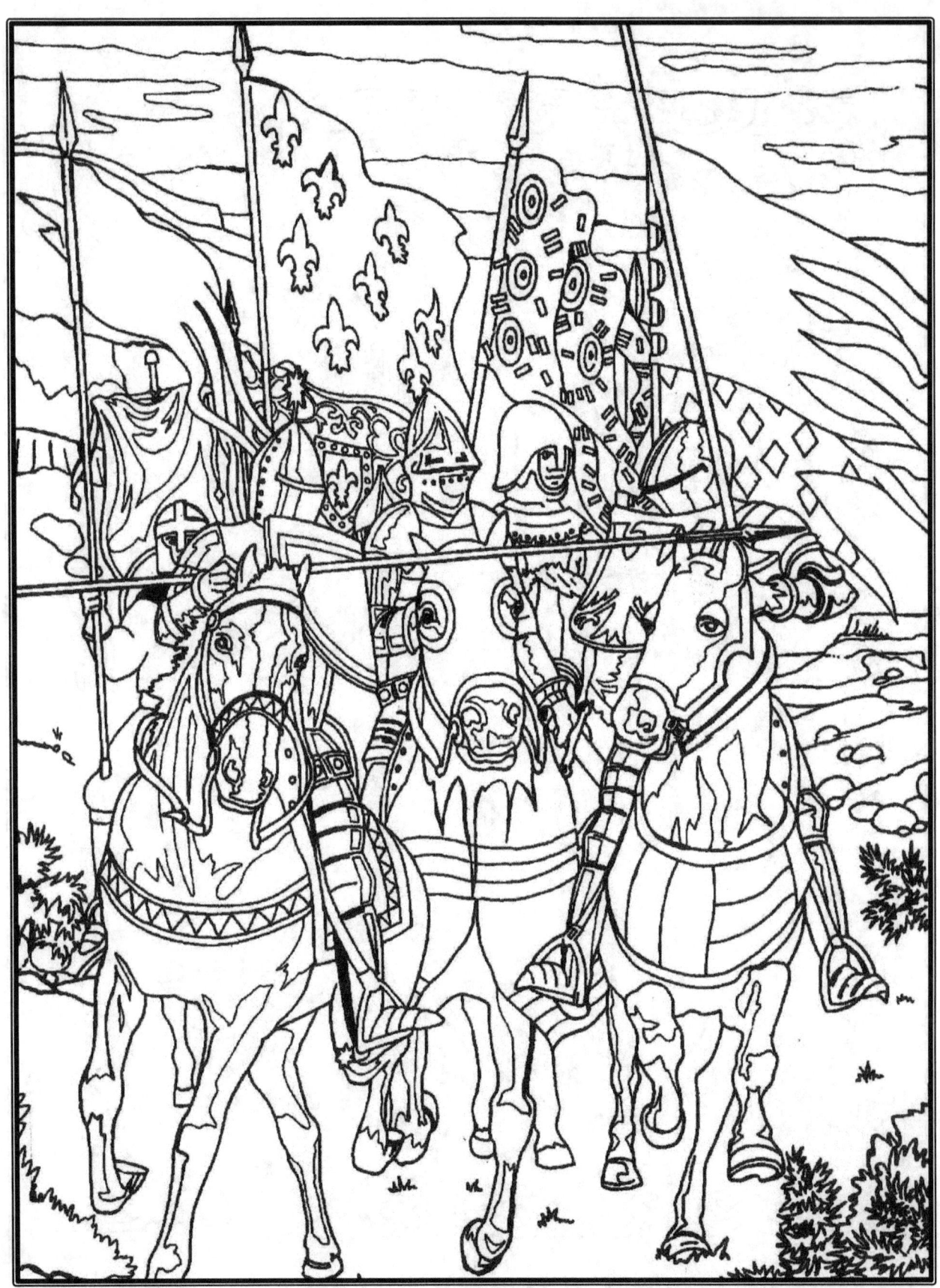

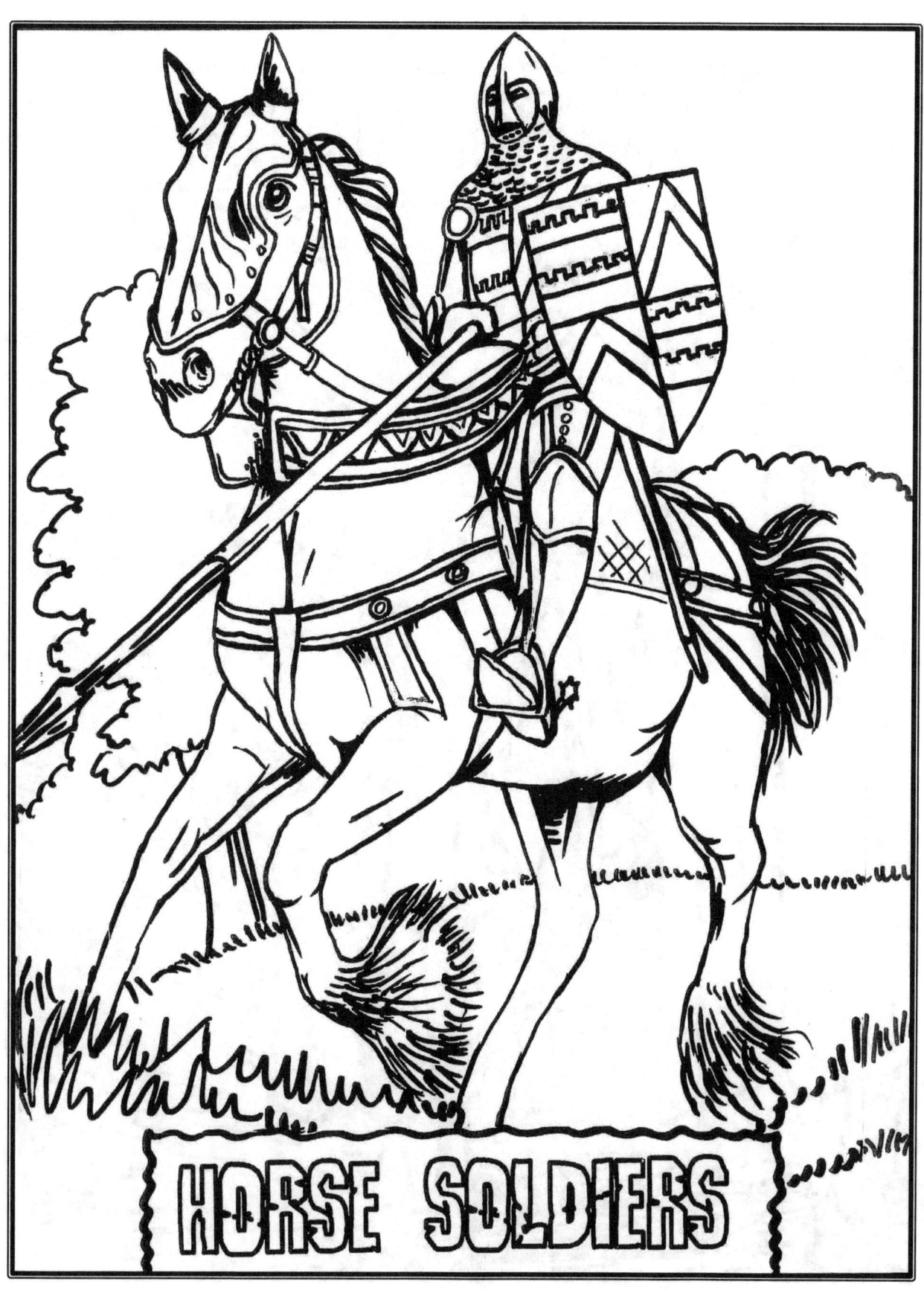

HORSE SOLDIERS

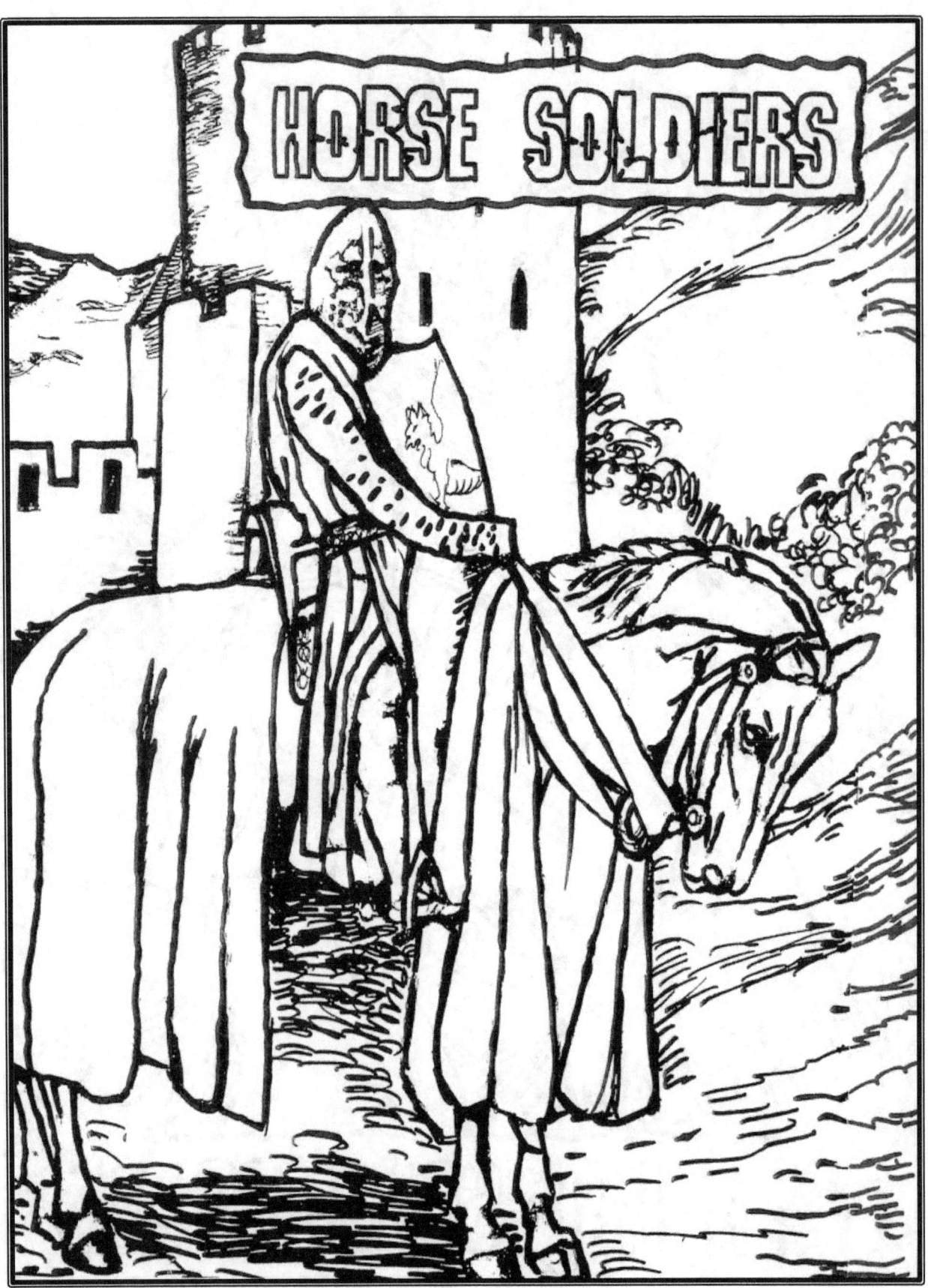

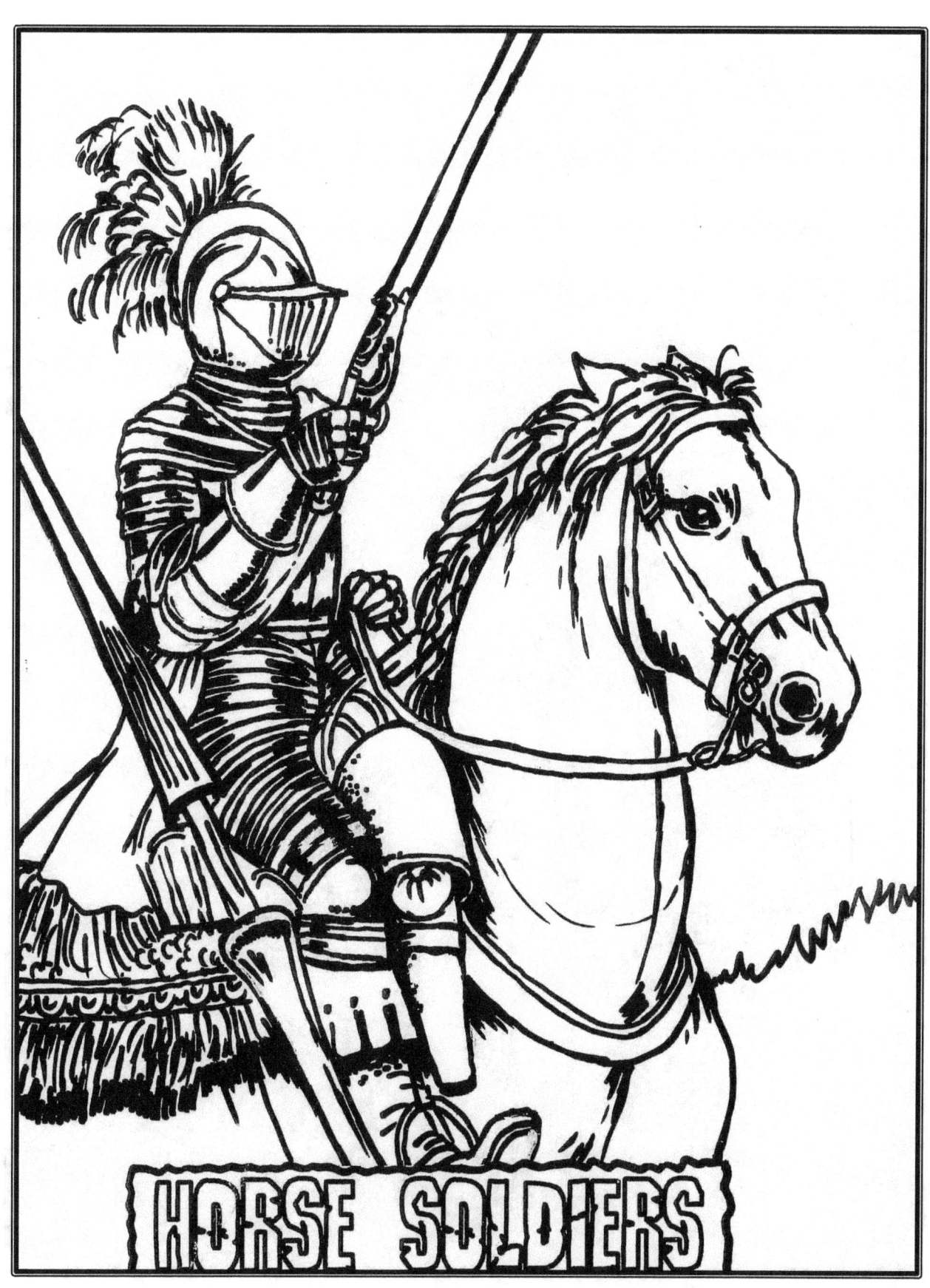

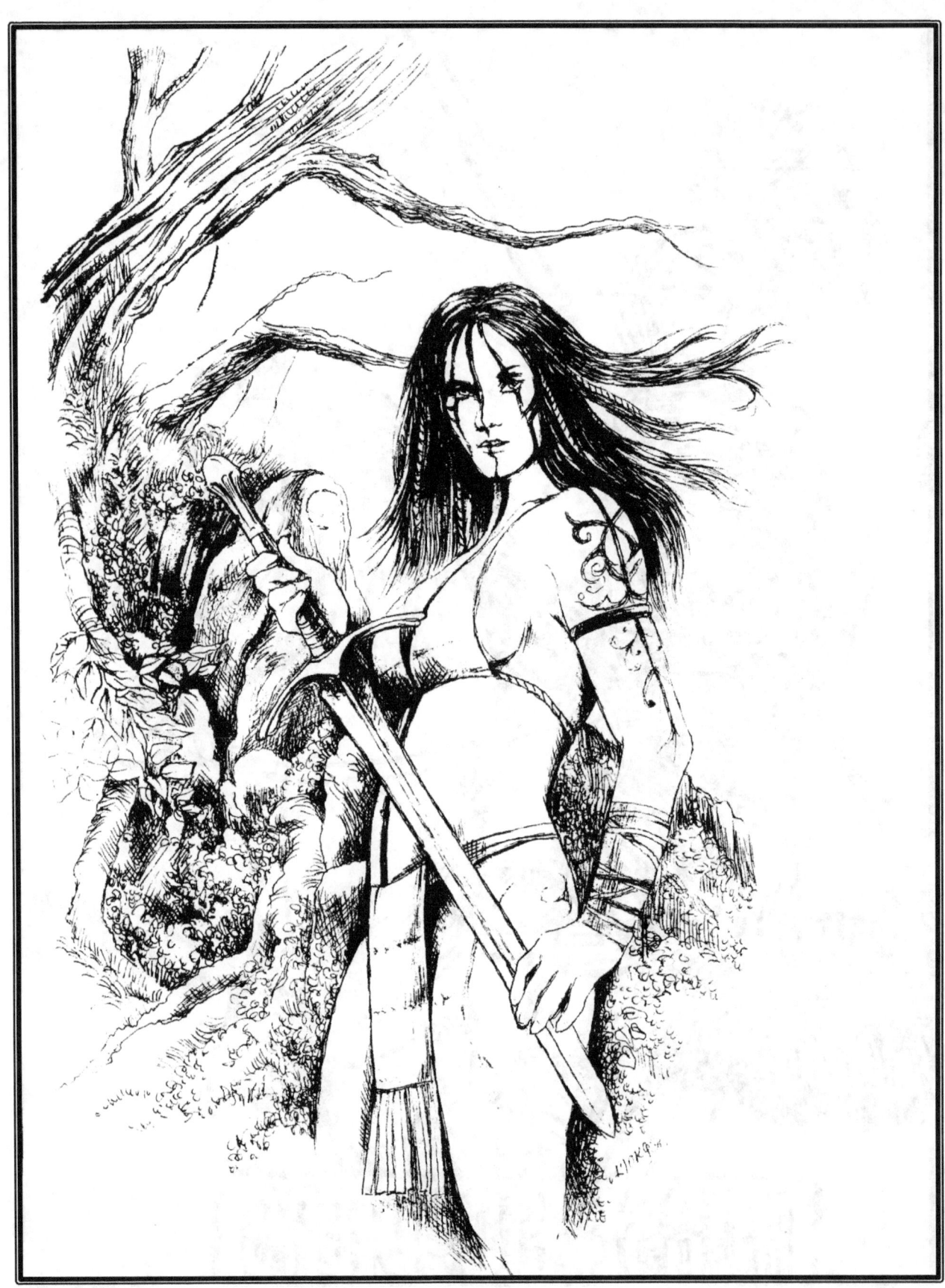

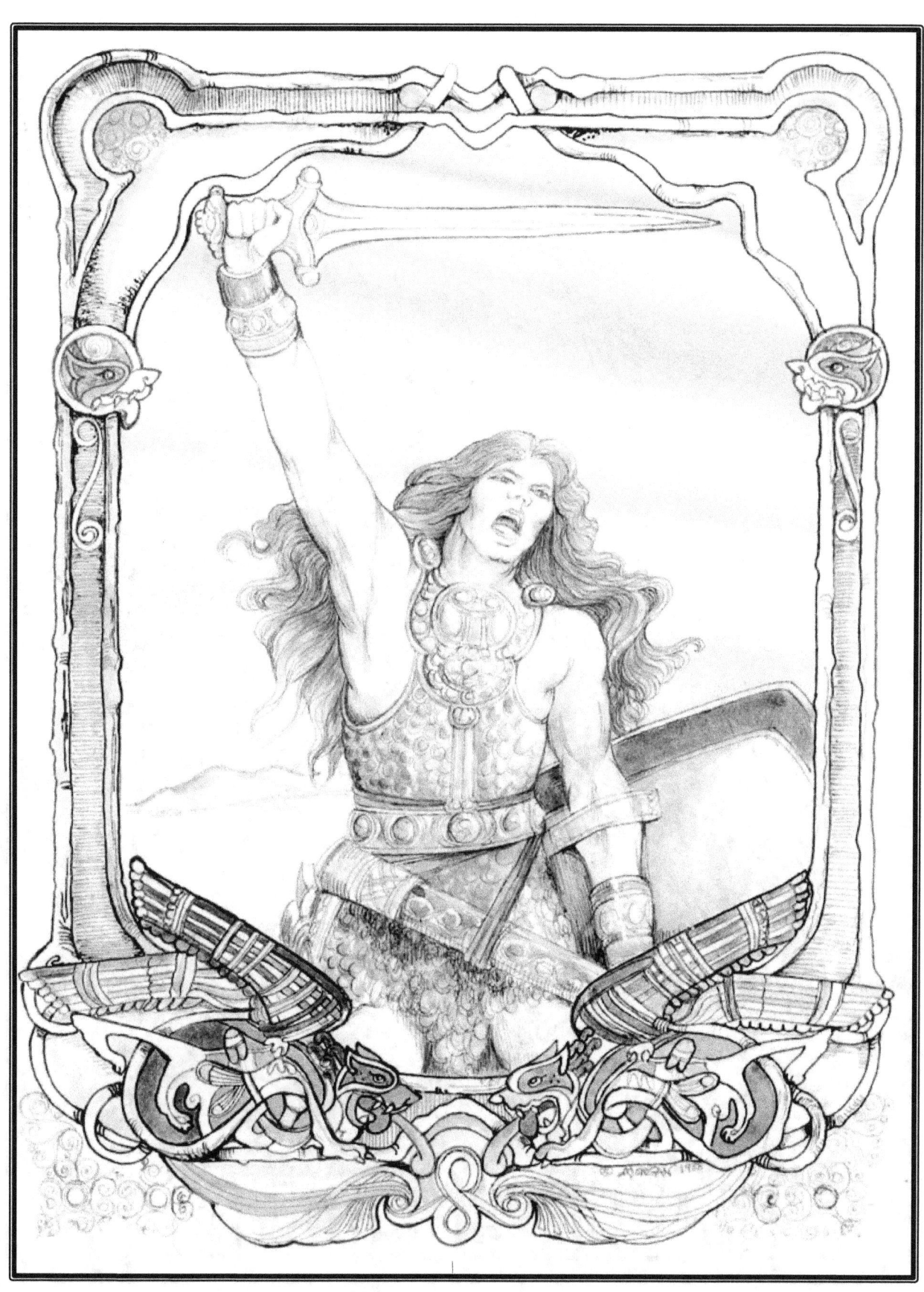

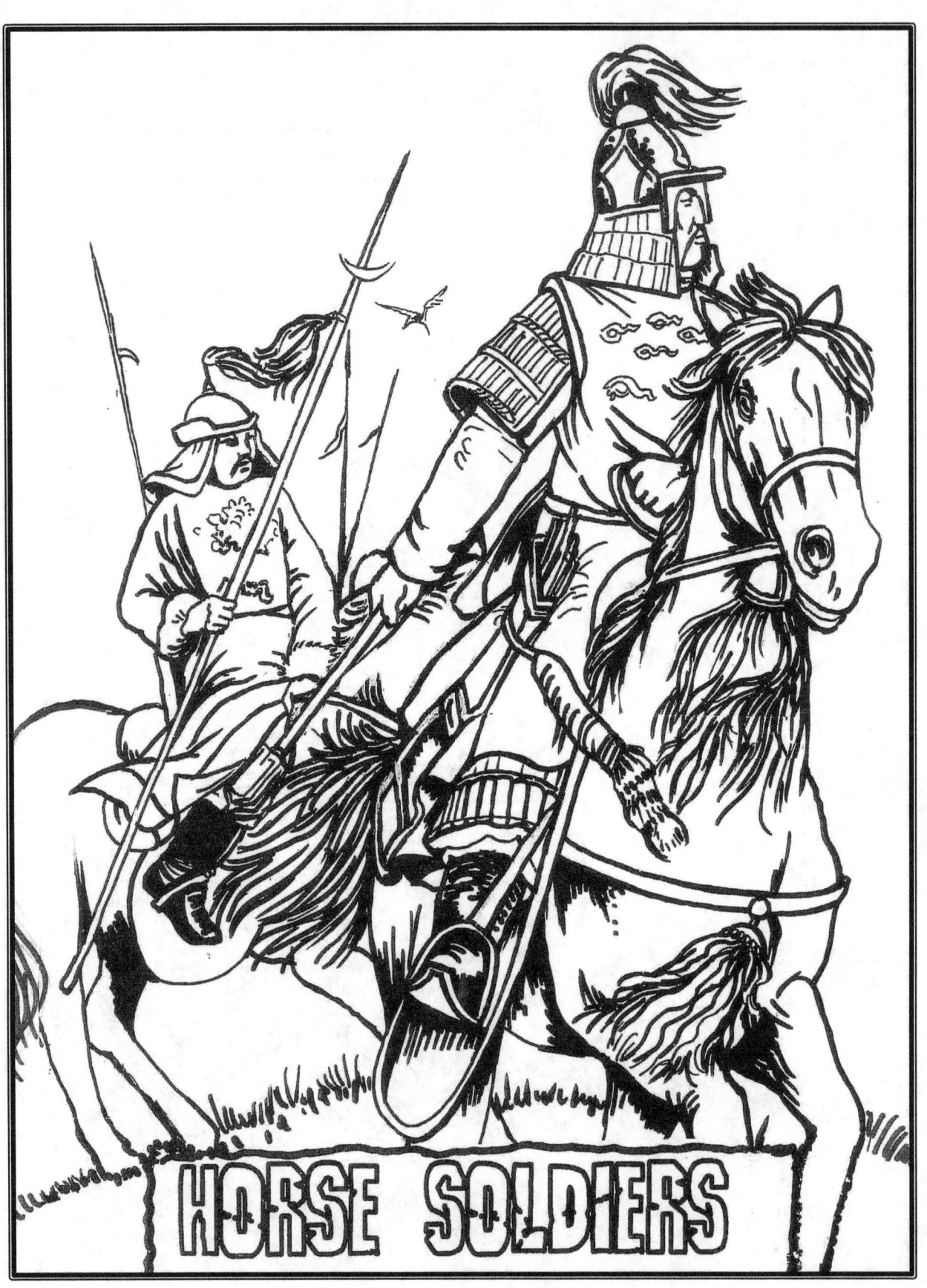

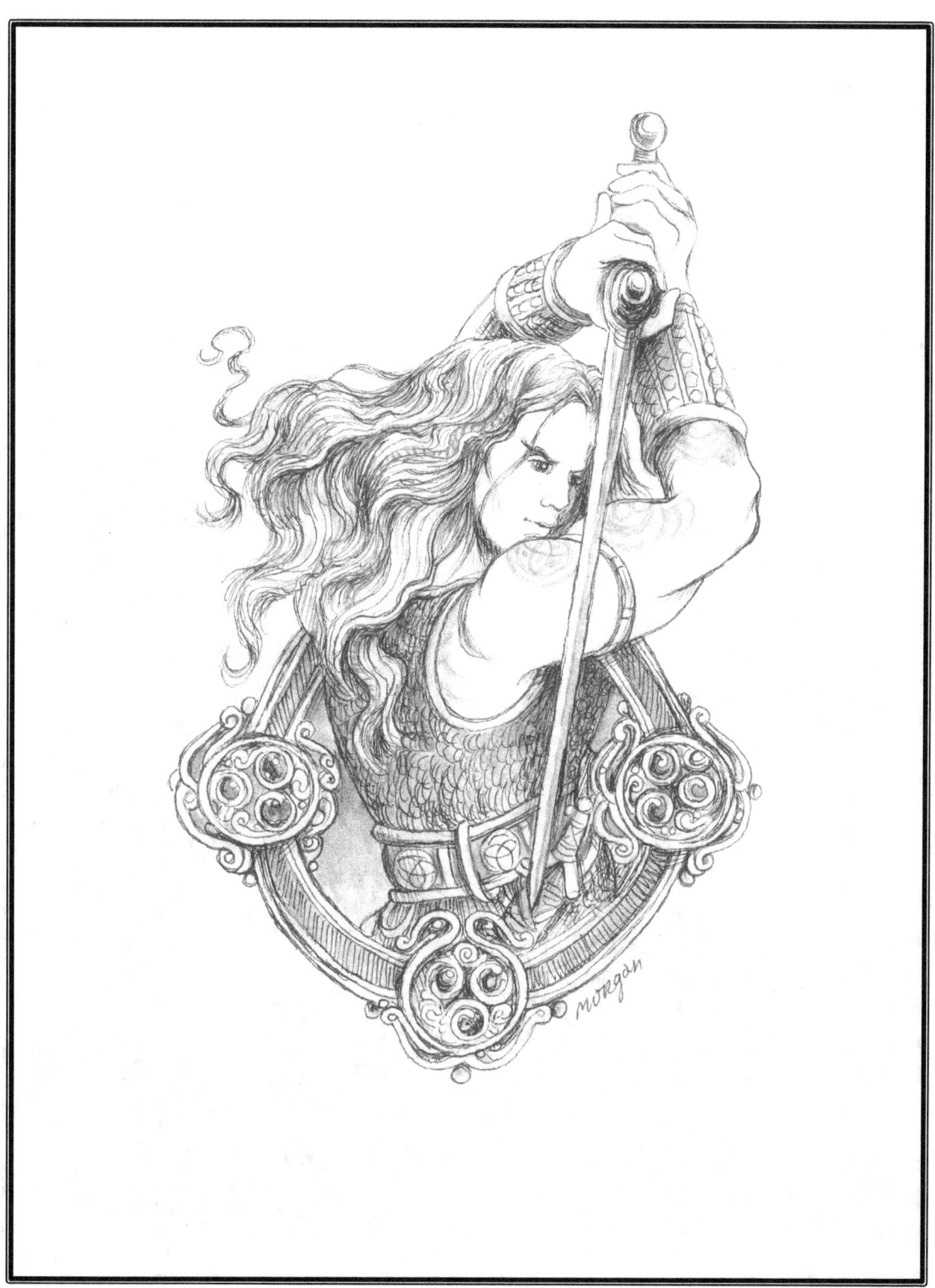

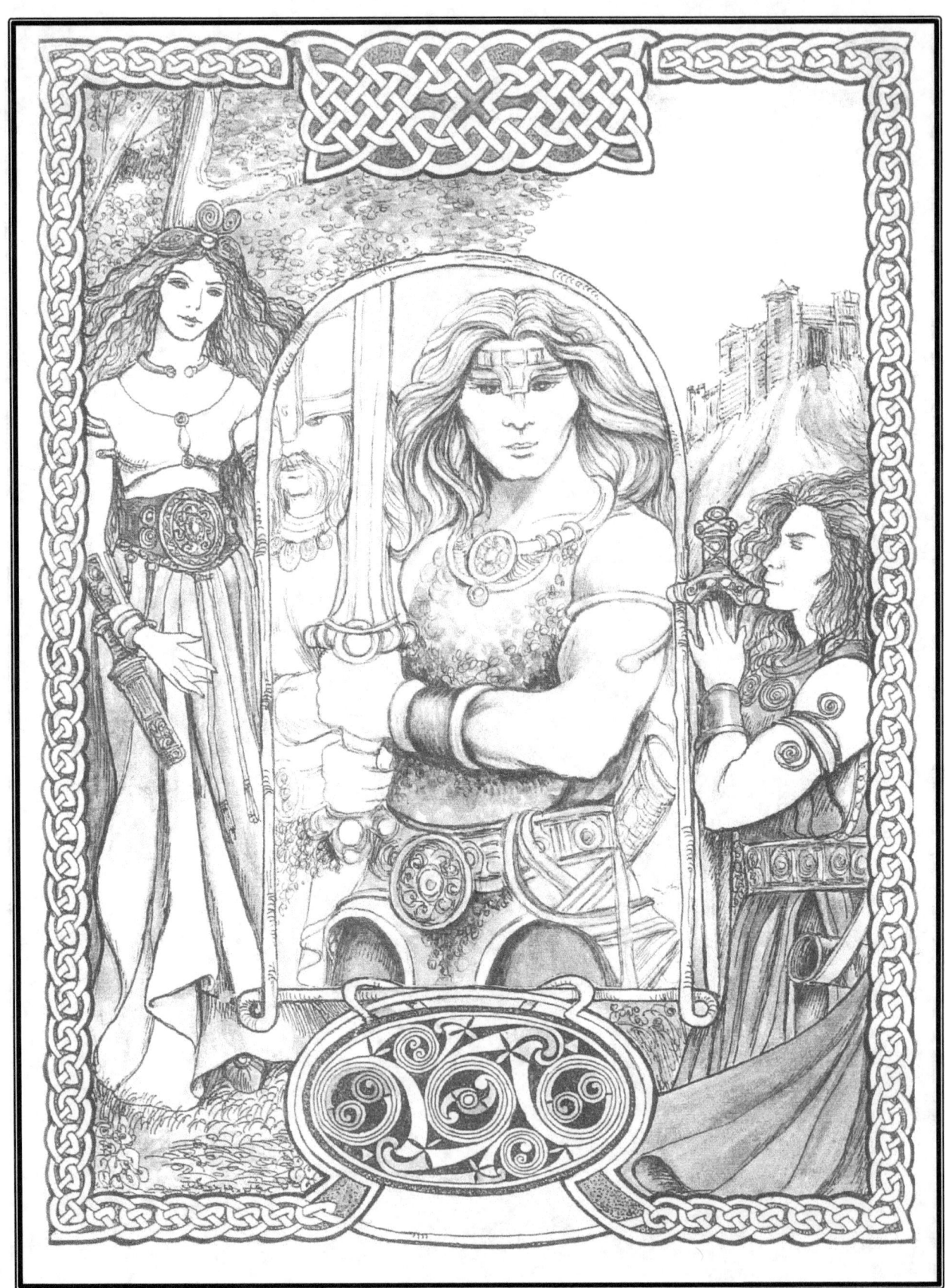

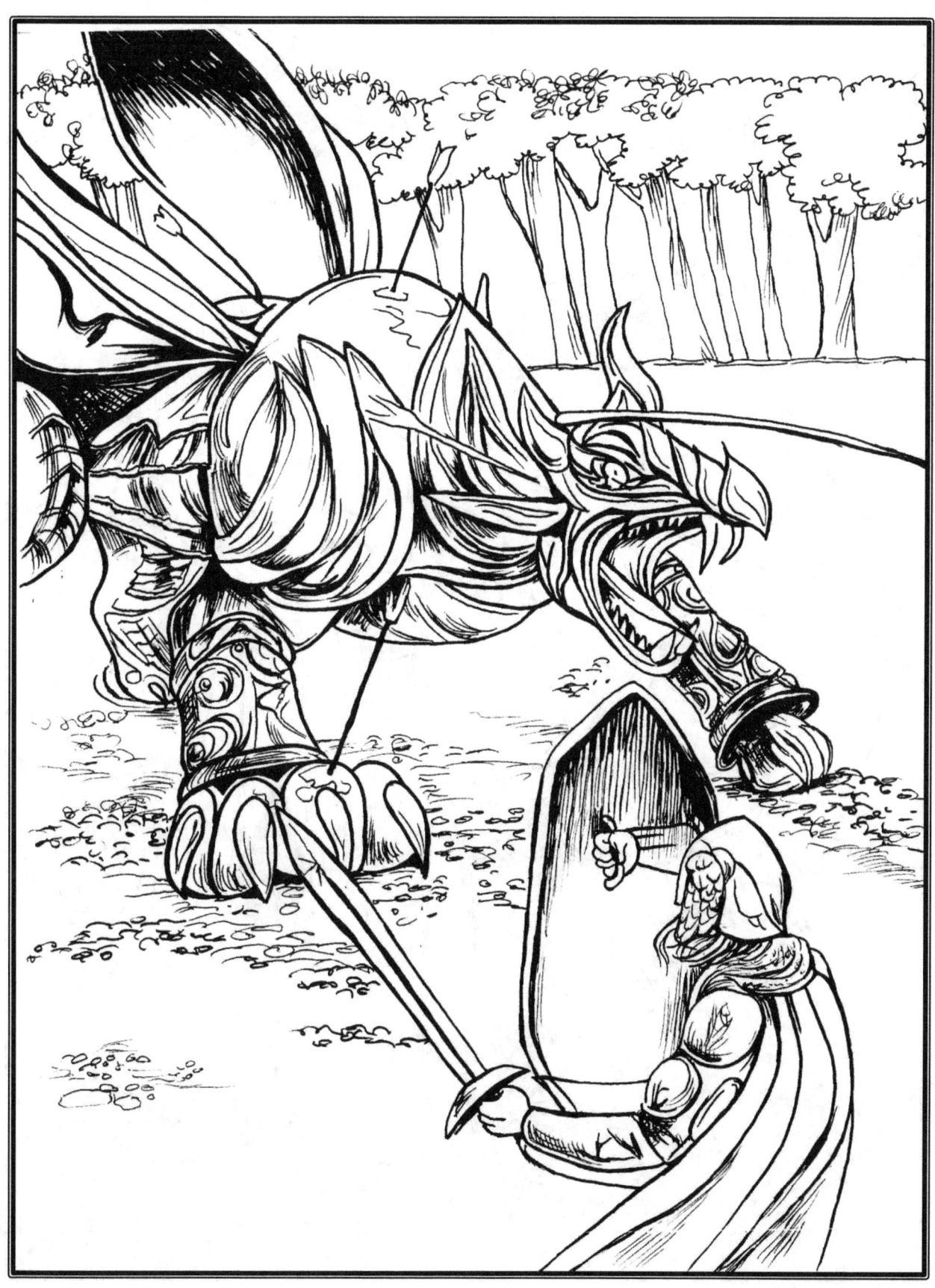

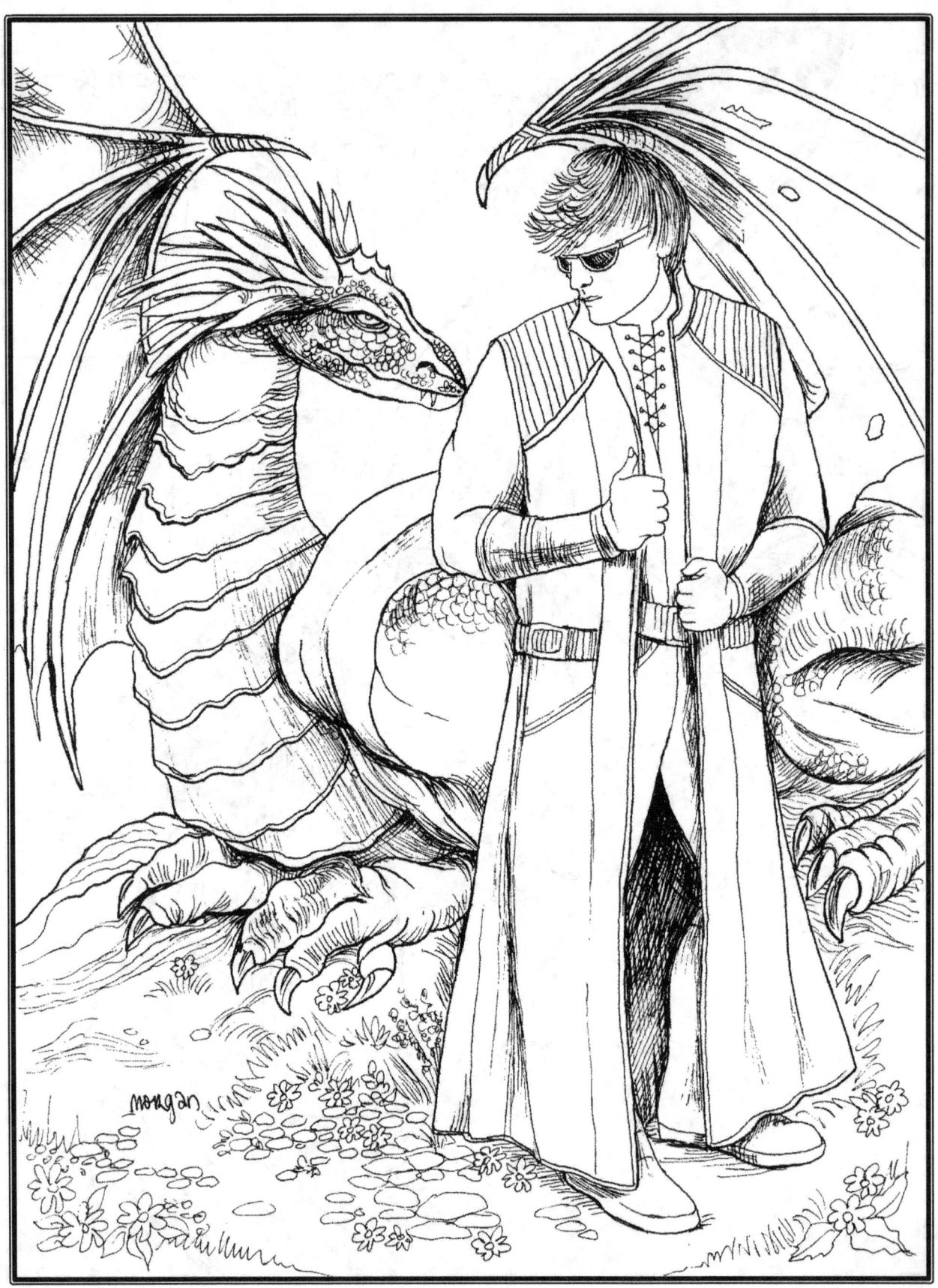

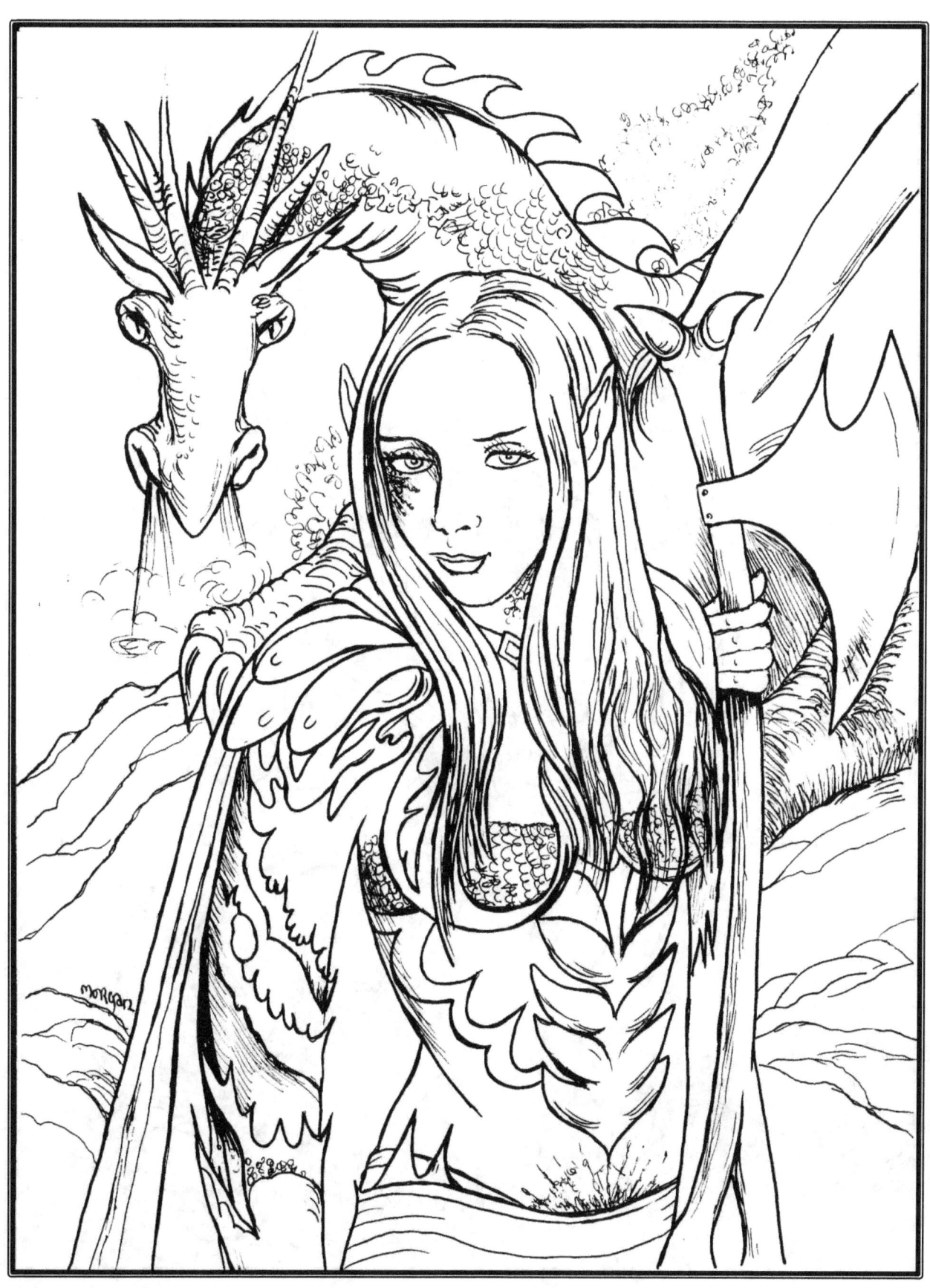

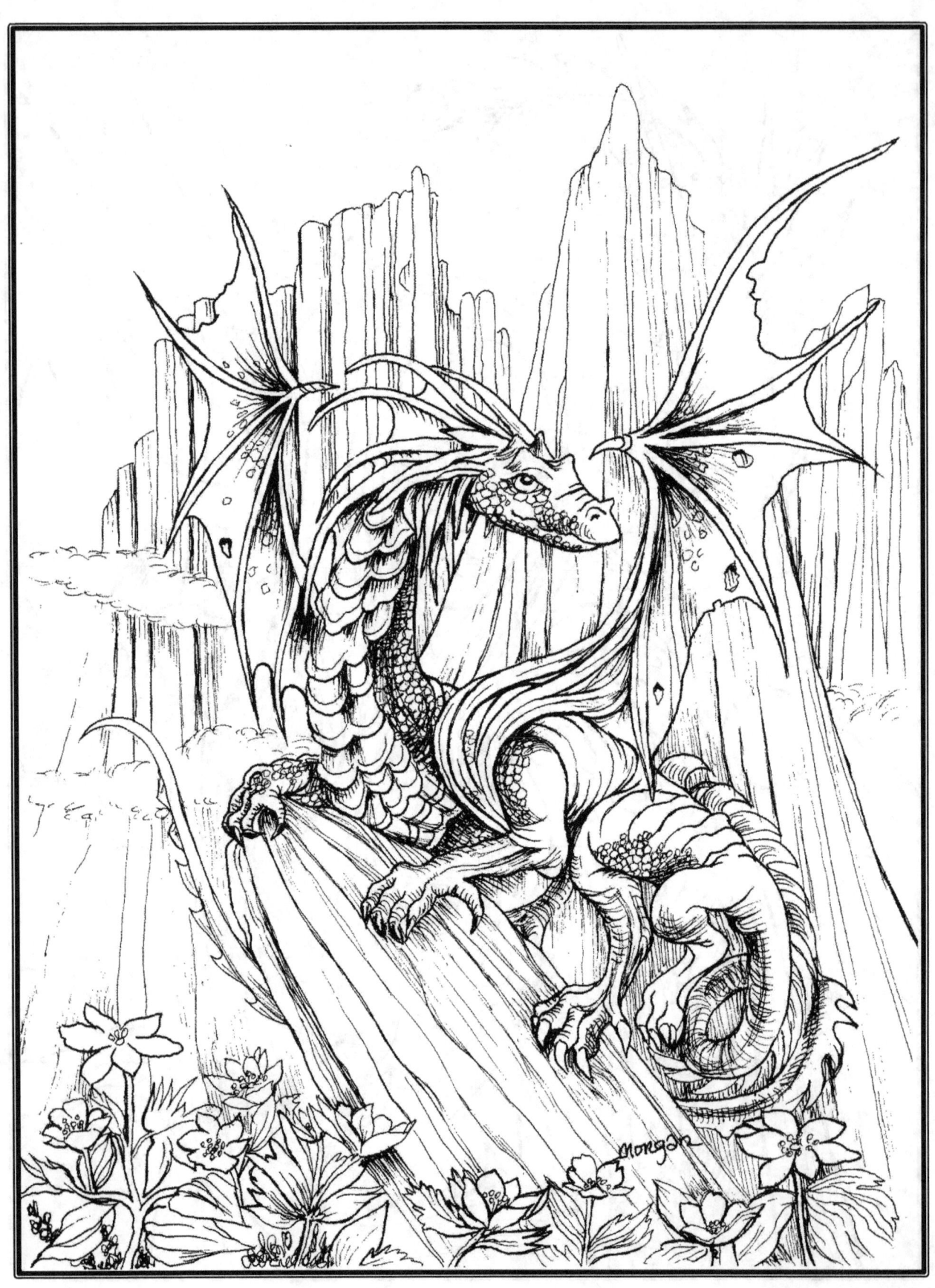

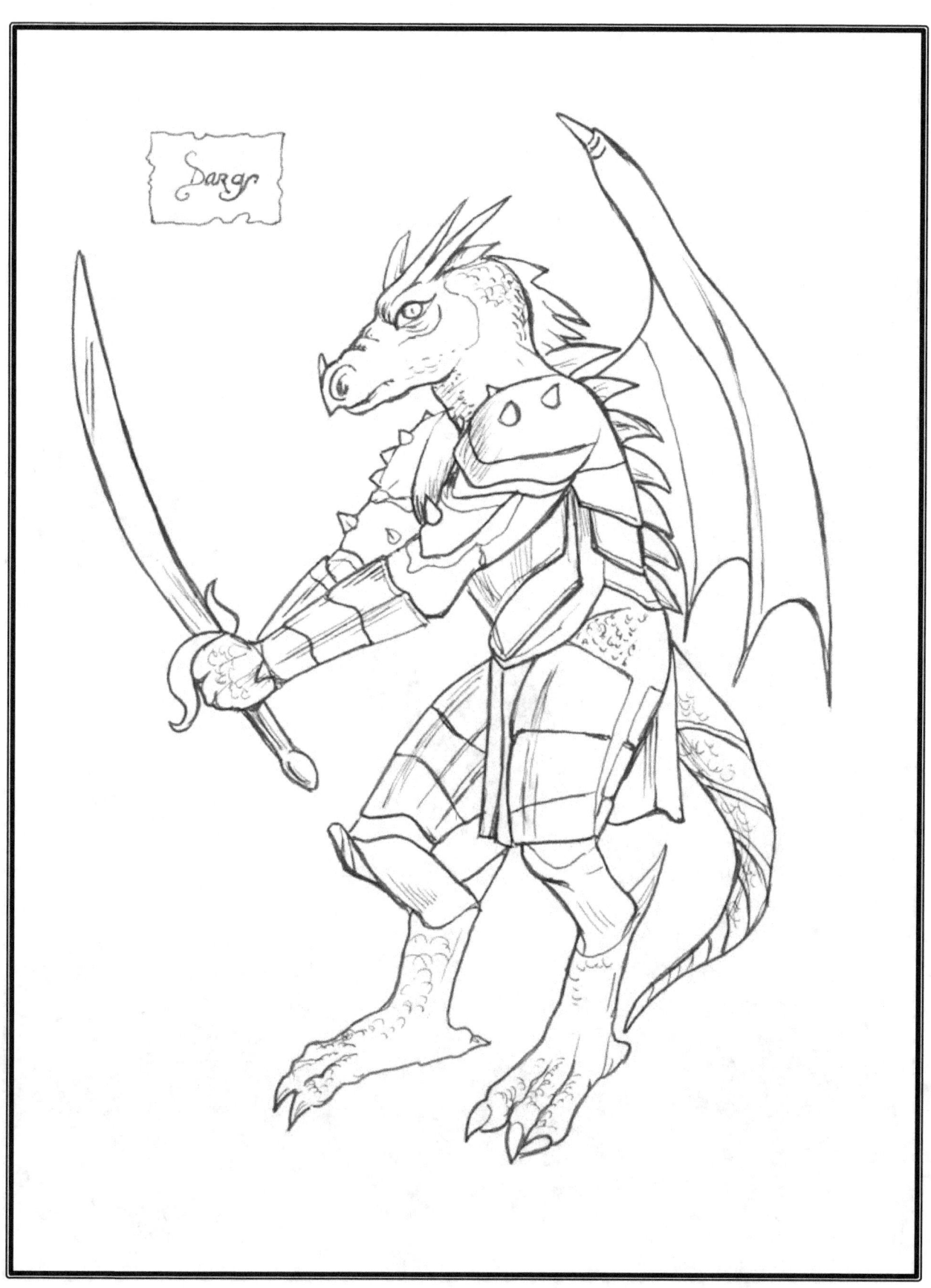

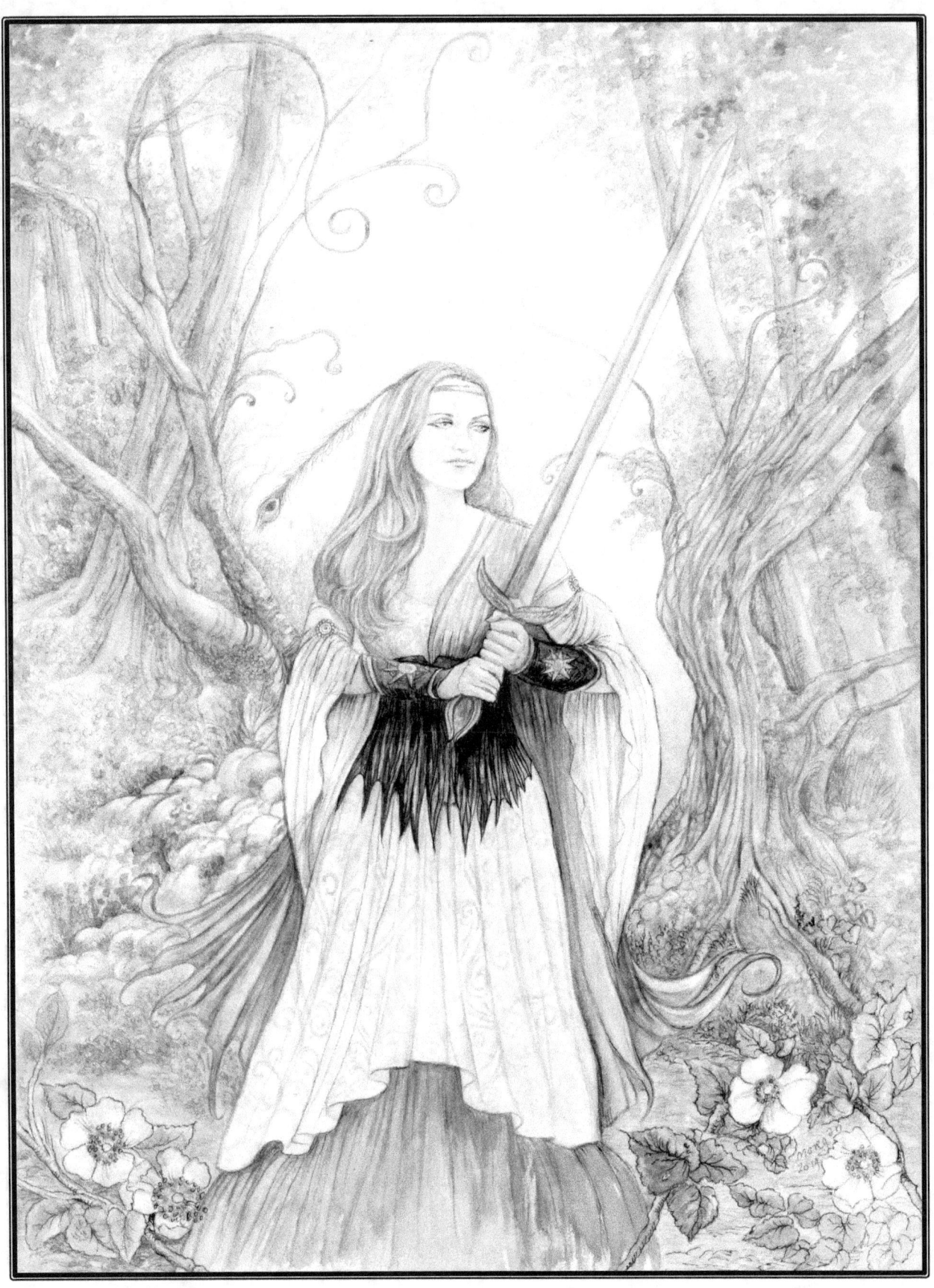

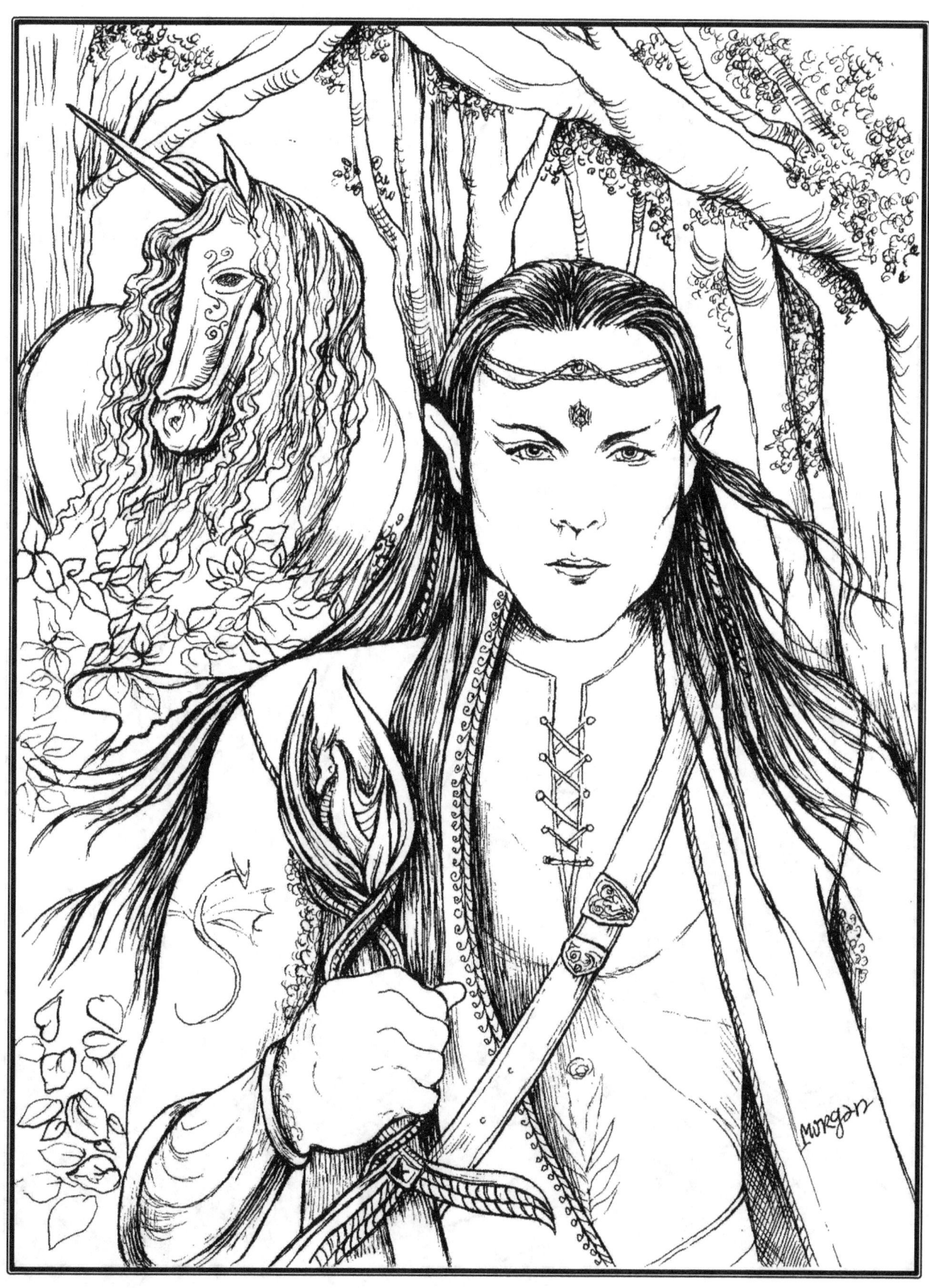

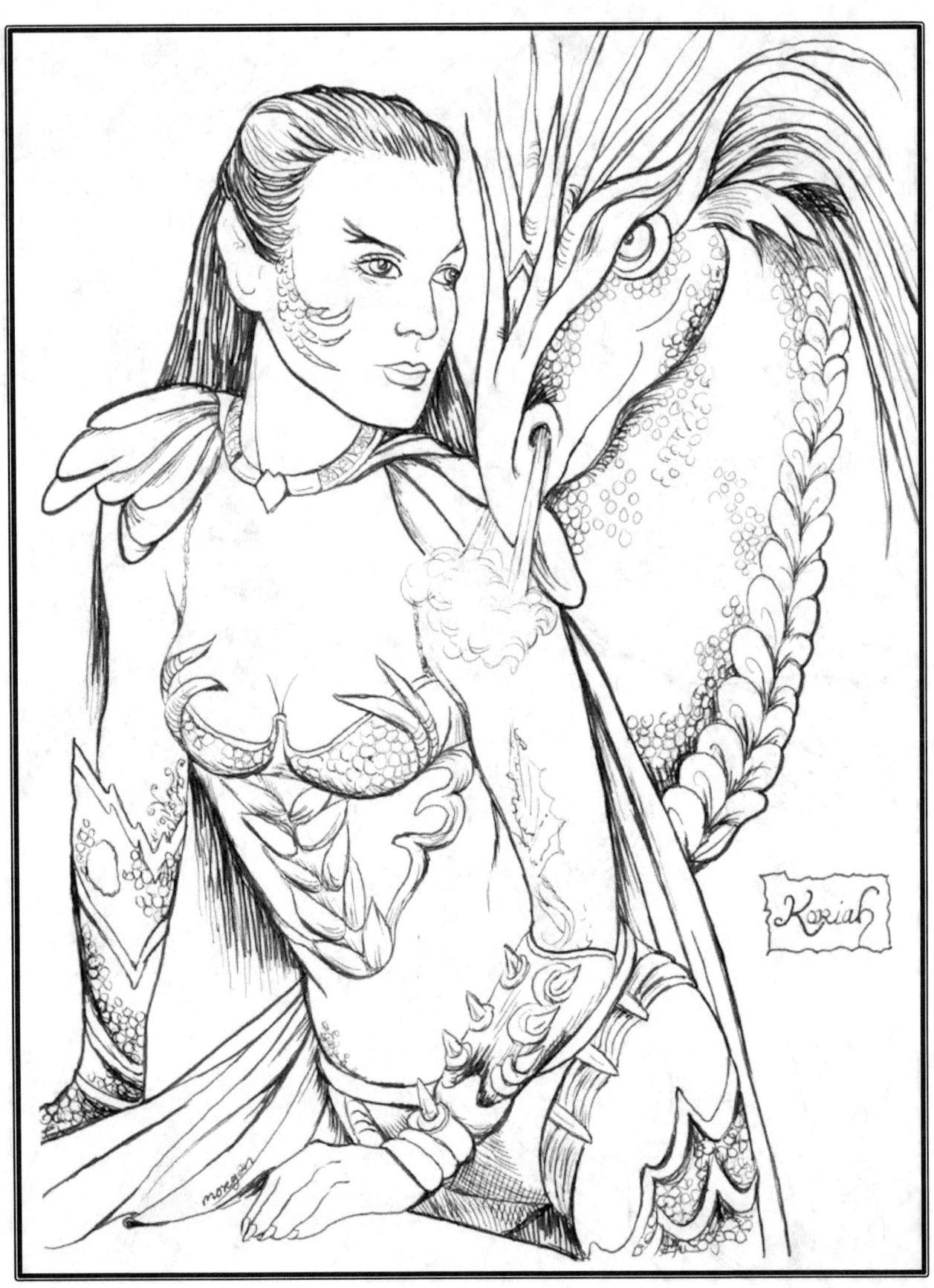

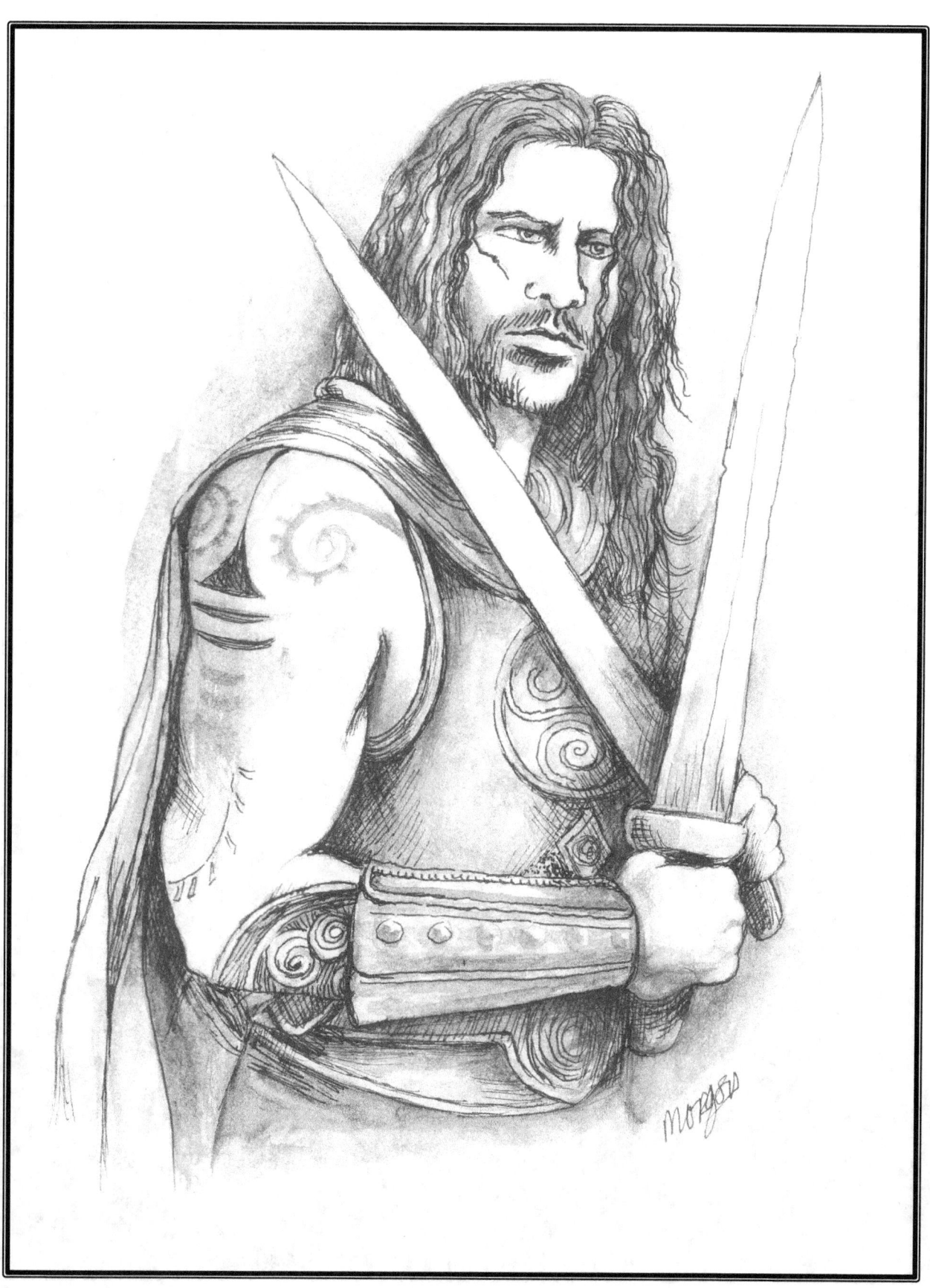

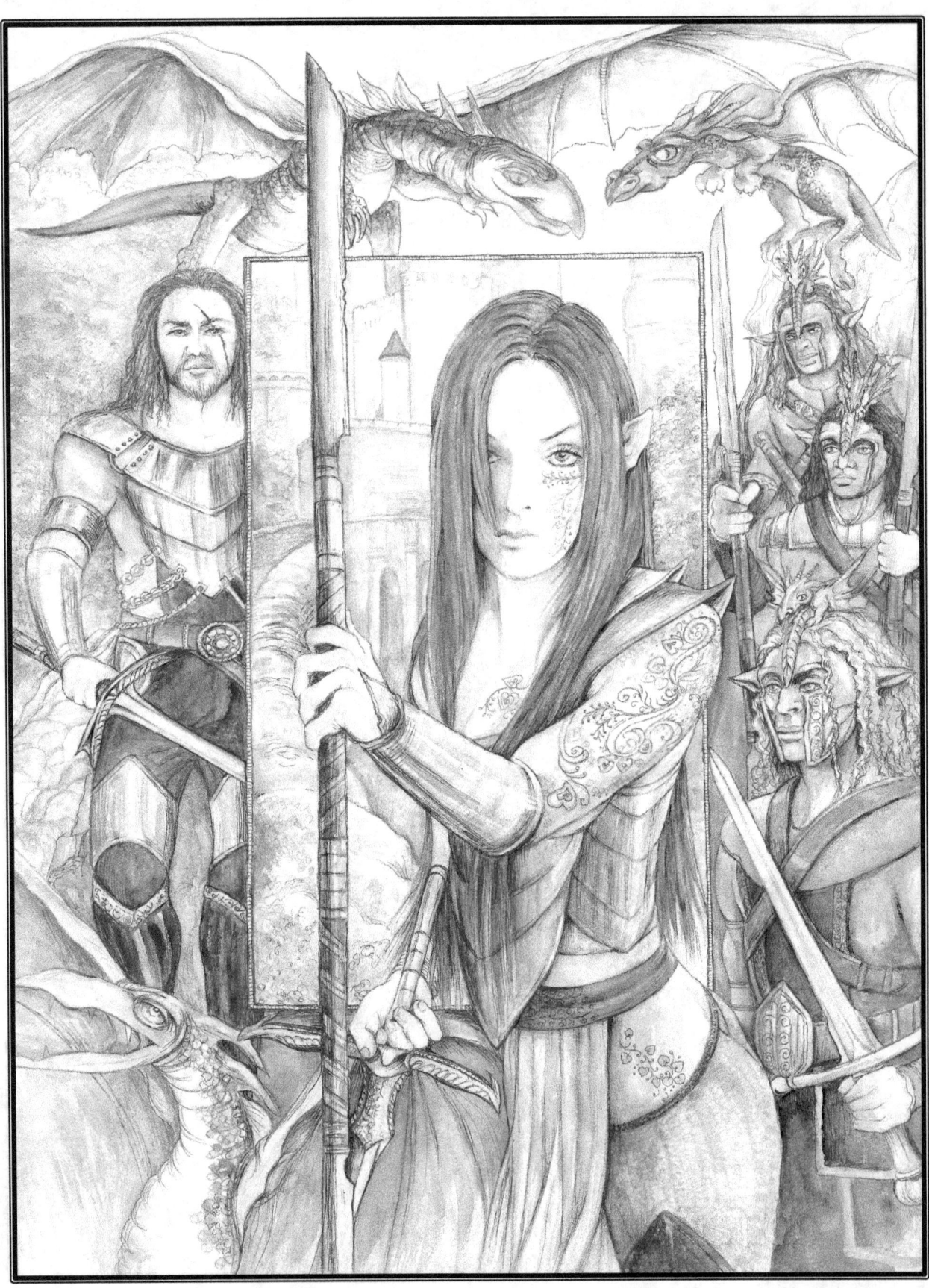

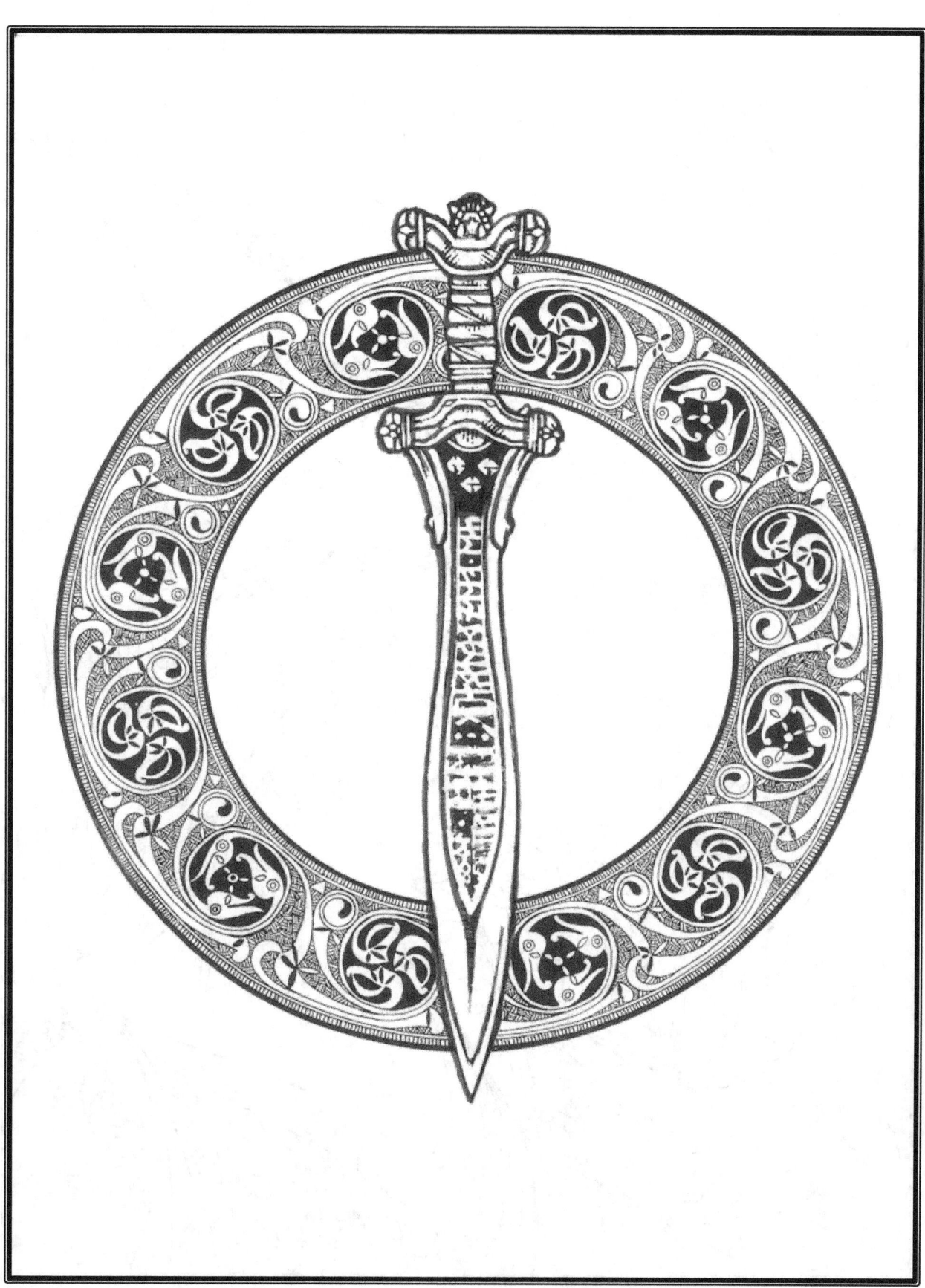

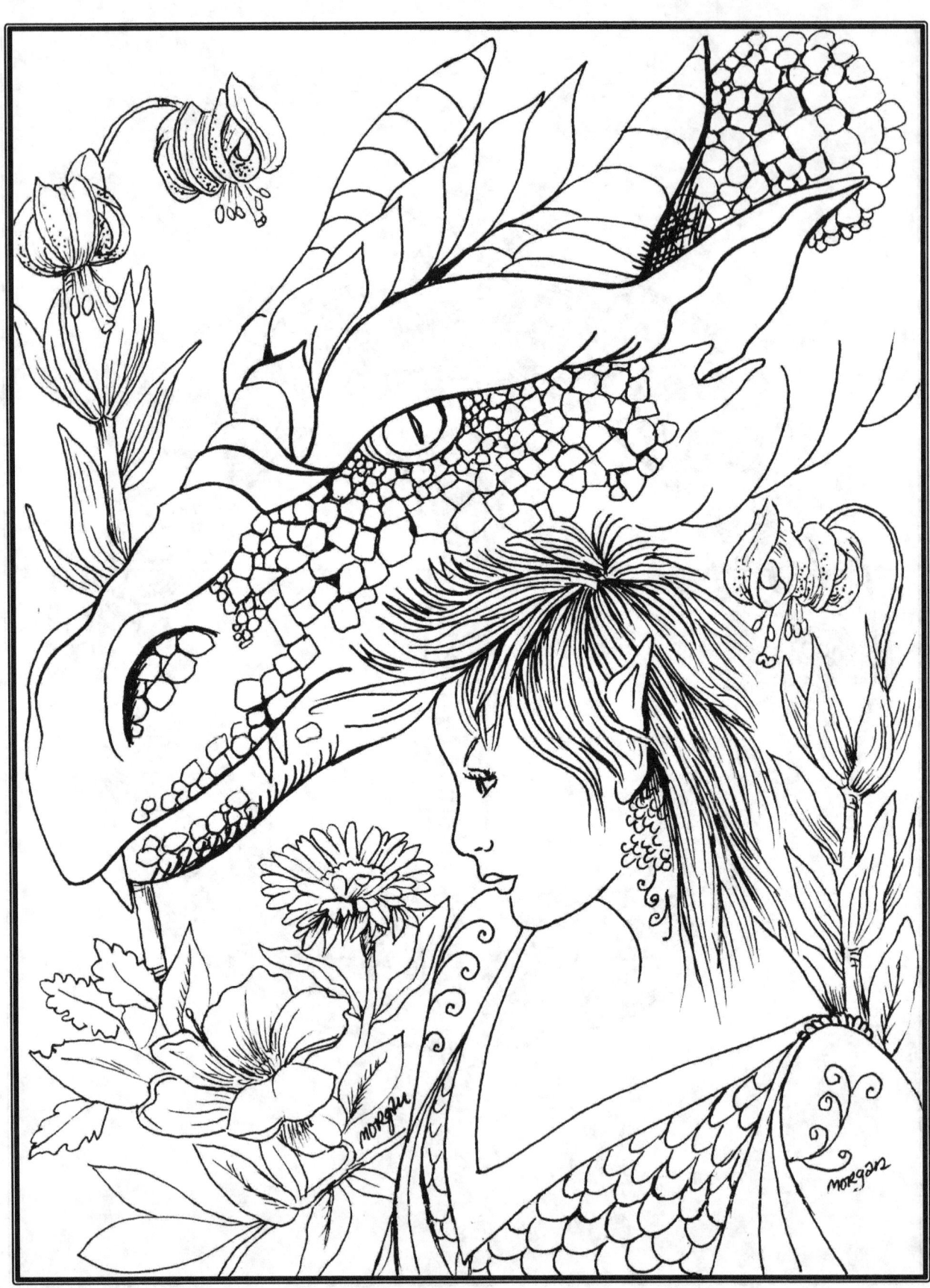

www.ingramcontent.com/pod-product-compliance
Lightning Source LLC
Chambersburg PA
CBHW081023170526
45158CB00010B/3137